THE COMPLETE IDIOT'S GUIDE® TO

Friendship
for Teens

Ericka Lutz

ALPHA

A Pearson Education Company

803

This book is dedicated to Tilly, who's taught me, since kindergarten, about friendship's depths.

Copyright © 2001 Ericka Lutz

Publisher: *Marie Butler-Knight*
Product Manager: *Phil Kitchel*
Managing Editor: *Jennifer Chisholm*
Acquisitions Editor: *Randy Ladenheim-Gil*
Development/Copy Editor: *Lynn Northrup*
Production Editor: *Billy Fields*
Illustrator: *Jody P. Schaeffer*
Cover Designer: *Dan Armstrong*
Book Designer: *Trina Wurst*
Layout/Proofreading: *Svetlana Dominguez, Susan Geiselman*

Contents at a Glance

Contents

Introduction

Friendship—it's an essential part of life. It's also a part of life you usually don't think a lot about. After all, you've probably been making friends from the time you could walk.

Even though friendship is a daily, common thing, friendship's skills—the art and craft of choosing, making, and keeping your friends—are too important to ignore. Friendship doesn't have to be hard work, but good friendships do require attention. Maybe you want to meet new friends, or you want to make more friends. Maybe you want better friends, or you want to learn how to be a better friend. Maybe you're having trouble with the friends you have, or you have a friend in trouble and don't know how to help. This book is written for you.

What's in the Book?

The Complete Idiot's Guide to Friendship for Teens is divided into three parts:

In **Part 1, "What Is a Friend?"** we'll start at the beginning, look closely at friendship and its purposes, then move into the skills involved in making new friends, being friends with yourself, and keeping your friendships strong and valuable.

In **Part 2, "Friendship in All Forms,"** we'll hone in on the many varieties of friendship, including best-friendship, friendship in groups (oh, those cliques!), long-distance and virtual friends, and friendships between guys and girls and the joys and complications that brings.

Finally, in **Part 3, "The Challenges of Friendship,"** we get to the harder and scarier parts of friendship. You'll learn how to deal with the friendship/romance combo, about "crimes" that poison friendships, how to effectively resolve conflicts, what to do when your friend is in crisis, and how to deal with the end of a friendship.

Friendly Acknowledgments

No book, especially a book about friendship, is ever written without a lot of help. I want to thank the ever-supportive Andree Abecassis,Randy Ladenheim-Gil, the Ginzu-knife-wielding Lynn Northrup (operating with surgical skill), and my Rhetoric 2B class at UC Berkeley, Fall 2000. *Merci* forever to the Writergirls, the Wild Plum plums, Dr. Susan Rabens, Johanina Wikoff, my parents Arthur and Karla Lutz, and my daughter Annie. A special shout to my teen advisors, including Liliana Lopez, Alicia Koester, Marcus Avila, Malancha Ghosh, Sopheary Khlok, and especially Uyen Nguyen (otherwise known as Lucky), who read huge chunks of this book and gave great feedback.

And, of course, I want to forever thank my friends, especially my one-'n-only-guy Bill and my gal pals Tilly, Ami, Saill, Milo, Laura, Susan, and Big Annie.

Trademarks

All terms mentioned in this book that are known to be or are suspected of being trademarks or service marks have been appropriately capitalized. Alpha Books and Pearson Education, Inc., cannot attest to the accuracy of this information. Use of a term in this book should not be regarded as affecting the validity of any trademark or service mark.

Part 1

What Is a Friend?

Let's begin at the beginning. What is friendship, anyway, and why do we need it? How do we get it? How do we keep it? This part looks at friendship's not-so-simple basics. Chapter 1 looks at the importance and purpose of friendship. Chapter 2 gives you tips and techniques for making new friends. In Chapter 3, we'll focus on one of the most important friendships you'll ever have: your friendship with yourself. And in Chapter 4, you'll learn in-depth skills for maintaining strong friendships.

Chapter 1

Friendship: The Incredible Bond

In This Chapter

- Friendship comes in all flavors
- Why do we need friends?
- Six key things friends provide
- Choosing your friends—one, two, or a group?

Friendship—it's important stuff! You're reading this book because you want to learn how to make friends, keep friends, become better friends, deal with friends in groups or one-on-one, argue brilliantly with friends ....

These are the skills involved in friendship, and that's the real focus of this book. But before you learn the fine art of friendship, it helps to think about friendship as a concept. What is a friend? What's so important about friends? How do we choose our friends? That's what we'll talk about in this chapter.

Acquaintance, Pal, "Sibling," Confidante, Life-Sharer

Friendship means something a little different to each person, but here's the dictionary definition: A friend is one attached to another by affection or esteem. In other words, friends are people who like and respect each other.

Friendship also comes in a wide variety of "flavors": friends you know casually, friends you play sports with, friends you call in an emergency, friends you squabble with like siblings, friends you can count on for life. And friendships can evolve: The kid you used to skateboard with in middle school might become your calculus buddy a few years later.

Just Between Friends

The concept of friendship differs around the world. In the Bangwa tribe in the African country of Cameroon, for example, friends are just as important (or more important) than family. Friends celebrate their anniversaries, exchange gifts, and publicly commit to another year of friendship.

The Importance of Friends

What's so great about friendship? Why do we need friends, anyway? It's simple. Having friends is good for your mental health and, oddly enough, your physical health, too. People with friends tend to stay healthier and live longer than people who don't have friends.

Having supportive friends helps you …

- Feel good about yourself and the world.
- Feel connected socially to a group of others.

And here's a bonus: Kids and teens who have good friendships usually go on to have good romantic relationships.

True-Life Friends

"Without friends, life would never be the same. Friendships play a role in a lot of the experiences you face in life."

—Sopheary, age 18

Psychologists say friendship gives people six basic things:

- **Companionship.** Loneliness is a universal human emotion. We all get lonely, even in a crowd! Or you may sit alone in your room just aching for somebody to talk to who really understands you. A friend is somebody to hang with, do things with, share experiences and adventures with.

- **Stimulation.** A friend is entertaining, interesting, exciting, and somebody to learn from. You each bring your own personality, knowledge, and life story to the friendship. By sharing who you are, how you were raised, how you do things, and what you know, you stimulate each other to change and grow.

- **Physical support.** A friend can give you a ride, help you braid your hair, work with you on your homework. You might bail a friend out if, for instance, she's promised to bake two dozen cookies for a club meeting, and doesn't know how to turn on the oven.

- **Ego support.** Feeling low? A friend lets you know you're worthwhile even when you're feeling like moldy mac and cheese. Friends build up each other's self-images. You need to know that you're wonderful, and a friend can help do that for you. (After all, when somebody as cool as your friend thinks you're the coolest, how could he be wrong?)

- **Social comparison.** You learn about yourself, and where you fit in socially, by looking at your friends. This one is touchy, but true. Your friends—the kids you hang out with—give you a sense of who you are. Who's smarter, cuter, stronger, cooler, meaner, calmer? Competing with your friends doesn't feel good, but comparing yourself with them is human. (There's more about comparing, not competing, in Chapter 4, "Friendship's Skills.")

- **Intimacy and affection.** Remember the definition of "friend": somebody attached to you by affection. Real friendship is a tight relationship. Who do you tell your secrets to? Who knows you better than anybody, except maybe your parents? Who giggles with you, slaps your shoulders, gives you a hug when you're feeling low? Who do you help solve problems with? Who's got your back?

Just Between Friends

Friends provide a sense of security. (Is that why girlfriends all seem to go to the bathroom in groups?)

Friendship, Great and Grueling

Friendship is terrific for a million and one reasons, but it can also be heartbreaking. We depend a lot on our friends, and when things go wrong or you and your friend fight, a friendship can be torn apart.

With family, you're sisters (or brothers or cousins or parent and child) for life. You have to work things out. A friendship is optional—just as we choose our friends, we can (and sometimes do) choose to *stop* being friends. In Part 3, "The Challenges of Friendship," we'll get to the tough sections.

So Many Friends, So Little Time ...

Okay, enough with the psychologists and the gloomy thoughts, let's get back to you. Friends can come one at a time, as one special person (more about this in Chapter 5, "The Best Friend"), or they come in cliques and crowds (we'll talk about this in Chapter 6, "Life in the Group of Friends"). How many friends do you need? Should you concentrate on making one friend or a group of them?

If you want to make new friends, start with one. Go for quality over quantity. One good friend is worth 20 "well, they're not *too* boring" acquaintances. A lot of the time, new friends come with other friends, and pretty soon you'll be friends with a group. It may take a while before you know if a new friend will become a best friend (most don't), but hey, not all friends have to be best friends! And not all friends require the same amount—or type—of time commitment.

Just Between Friends

We all have many different qualities and interests, and it's really rare that one friend can satisfy all our needs or be interested in all the things we're interested in. If you have a lot of friends, each can play a different role in your life. Each friend can reflect different sides of your personality.

Who Will You Choose?

When you were a kid, you probably didn't really choose your friends, they became your friends by default. Many of the kids in your class were your friends because you saw them every day. The kids who lived in your neighborhood became your pals. Sure, you got along better with some kids than others, and maybe you even formed special bonds with some, but often you didn't have a lot of choice in the matter.

Teens, on the other hand, get to pick their own friends. How do you choose? Picking and making friends lets you think about what you like in people, what you respect, and who you want to hang out with. Not everybody you meet will become a friend, and that's cool.

Friendship occurs between people who have common interests and values, who like the same types of activities, and who share a sense of intimacy. Why do people hang with people who are like them? Well, simply put, friends tend to have a lot in common.

A Friendly Reminder

Your parents are right (at least about this): Friends do influence each other, especially in things like using drugs and alcohol. I'm talking peer pressure here!

Shopping for new friends gives you a chance to think a bit about your interests and values. Think about your existing friends. You're probably into a lot of the same things. You're likely in the same grade. You probably have similar levels of ambition. You might have similar plans for the future, and you probably feel much the same about drinking and smoking and sex. For girls, especially, friends often have a similar level of sexual experience. (Guys don't—but that's a whole different book!)

This doesn't mean you have to hang with people who are like you. Friends often have different personality types and self-esteem levels. How social you are and how gorgeous (or not) you are rarely seems to matter between friends. How well you get along with your parents doesn't seem to matter for most friends. Even intelligence doesn't seem to matter; a real brain might be best friends with somebody quite marginal in the thinking department.

So go on, break the mold! And while you're breaking it, remember to have fun. Because ultimately, that's what friendship is about, right?

The Least You Need to Know

- A friend is one attached to another by affection or esteem.
- Not all friends or types of friendship are the same.
- Friendship keeps you healthy, both emotionally and physically.
- Friends provide companionship, stimulation, physical support, ego support, and social comparison plus intimacy and affection.
- If you want to make new friends, start by making one; then branch out.
- Most friends share common interests and values, but don't limit yourself. Reach out to people who have different interests and backgrounds than your own!

Chapter 2

How to Make a Friend

In This Chapter

- Tips for getting over your shyness
- Five steps to making the friend you want
- Everyone you meet is a potential friend
- Finding opportunities to make new friends
- Opening yourself up and sharing confidences
- When it's not working out: letting go and trying again

This chapter is about the first part of friendship—making friends. Maybe you're very shy and have trouble making friends. Maybe you're new in town, or maybe things haven't been working out with your old gang and you're ready for some new blood. Perhaps you have a number of surface friendships, but nobody to really bond with. This chapter's for you.

Even if you have a lot of friends, this chapter is for you, too. I know, you like your friends, and you don't have time for any more. But before you start flipping the pages, think again. Friendships create happiness and satisfaction. Friends play many roles in life (you can review some of these roles in Chapter 1, "Friendship: The Incredible Bond"). Friends are a good thing—it's hard to have too many!

The Shy Factor

Most people are shy to a degree. But if you're painfully shy, it's harder for you to make the first move in a friendship, respond to others' overtures, or even realize that somebody is interested in being your friend. Taking care of yourself—befriending yourself, liking yourself, realizing fully what you feel, and knowing what you want (which we'll talk about in Chapter 3, "Finding the Friend Within Yourself")—can help you overcome shyness. Here are some other tips for battling shyness:

- Accept your shyness as a part of yourself. Once you do, you can work to change it.

- Pretend you are confident, bold, and very friendly, even if you don't feel that way. Stand tall and walk with your head held high. When your body takes on a confident look, your feelings will follow.

- When you feel that stomach-turning, hand-sweating shyness, allow yourself to admit it. Instead of concentrating on thinking, "I'm *not* shy," say the following affirmations to yourself: "The world is a gentle place," and, "I'm scared and shy but I'm confident and my shyness won't stop me."

- Write down some simple and direct lines (as though you're an actor) and practice saying them in the mirror. Try the friendly approach: "Hi! I'm Alonza, and I saw you yesterday at lunch time eating chocolate pudding. Want one of these cookies?" Or try the controversial approach (and get a discussion going): "Hi! I'm Alonza, and I saw you yesterday at lunch time eating chocolate pudding. How can you eat that stuff? I think the texture's disgusting."

- Remember to listen to what the person has to say. Boom, before you know it, you have a conversation going!

Five Steps to Making Friends

Friends don't always just show up in our lives, all dressed up and ready to play. If you want more friends, you need to go out and make them. Most of the time, we make friends instinctually. If you want to improve your friend-making powers, though, it helps to break this elaborate process down into five steps.

1. Broaden your horizons.
2. Be real—be friendly.
3. Recognize and pursue your opportunities.
4. Open up.
5. Try, try again.

Sure, it sounds simple, but it's harder in practice than on paper. Let's look at one step at a time.

Just Between Friends

Want to broaden your friendship network? Treat every person you meet as a potential friend, open your heart and mind, and relax your inhibitions.

Broaden Your Horizons

Step one to making new friends is broadening your horizons. This means meeting as many people as you can, and it means looking at everybody you meet as a potential friend.

True-Life Friends

"Just meet as many people as you can. Talk to everybody!"

—Kevin, age 16

Where can you find new friends? Look around you.

- School (in class and out)
- Your neighborhood or apartment building
- Afterschool activities
- Family friends
- Friends of friends
- Your local café
- Church or temple
- Online

A Friendly Reminder

Listen to the little voice in the back of your mind. Don't hang with strangers, especially those you meet online. Not everybody is safe or smart—and you know it.

Where there are activities, there are people, and where there are people, there are potential friends. Sharing activities with people gives you a chance to spend in-depth time with a small group so you really get to know the people. That's a great place to start.

Try each new activity at least four times. The first few times, you'll be nervous, on guard, and maybe intimidated by how friendly everybody is with each other. By time number four, you'll be a regular. You can't make friends (or even really figure out if there's anybody you're interested in being friends with) until you're relaxed.

Trying new activities never has to stop. For example, in the last two years I've checked out ...

- Book clubs.
- Sculpture classes.
- Ice-skating lessons.
- A bungee-cord dance class (you should have seen me hanging upside down in the air, trying to look graceful!).

I didn't try these activities just to make friends—but as a sideline, I certainly have. The big plus is that you'll be learning something new and having fun.

Just Between Friends

So you've joined three clubs and two teams and still haven't found anybody you really, really like? You're still exploring something really cool and having fun!

Be Real—Be Friendly

The second step to making new friends is to just be yourself and be friendly. In class, out of class, during afterschool activities, at your part-time job ... wherever there are people, you have opportunities to be friendly. Slow down. Venture a smile. Does somebody need a hand, a pen, a jumpstart? Give the world a break.

Be yourself. Friendliness goes nowhere if it's bogus. Neither does acting ultra-cool, wild, or sophisticated, especially if you're putting on an act. Your friends will like you for who you are, not for who you pretend to be, and pretending to be something you're not will get you absolutely nowhere.

True-Life Friends

"Don't try too hard. Don't sit there stressing about what to say to make people like you. Trust me, the more you try to be funny and 'cool' the less you'll be successful. You're not stupid, you're almost an adult—don't assume your peers won't see past the fake 'face' you put up."

—Lili, age 18

Recognize and Pursue Your Opportunities

So you've broadened your horizons, and you're meeting everybody in sight. Somewhere along the line you meet somebody who seems intriguing. Now it's time for the third step: to chat 'em up. This, for some people, is the hardest part. Okay, granted, it can feel like a big step from saying "Hi" and smiling to asking the person if she'd like to hang out with you. Making new friends is risky—yes, people may refuse your approaches—but if you don't make a move, you'll never know. Your move doesn't have to be particularly witty or brilliant. You just need to give the message, "Hey, you seem kind of interesting. Want to hang out?"

How do you know if you've found a potential friend? It's not always easy to tell. New friendships can either click right away or grow gradually. Sometimes it's like the Hollywood version of love: You look across a crowded room and BOOM! There he or she is ... and you suddenly get a mysterious feeling that you've known the person before, or that, even better, you just know that you need to, want to, and will get to know that person. Yes, friendship happens that way—sometimes.

True-Life Friends

"I remember clicking with Ami in third grade. She was the new girl, and she had wild curly hair, freckles, and killer cowboy boots. 'Wow,' I thought. At lunch time I sat next to her and offered her some of my pomegranate. 'Sure!' she said, shyly. We've been best friends ever since."

—Ericka

Of course, you don't need to feel that instant click to have the friendship be a real one. A friendship can also creep up on you. There's that guy who's been sitting near you in Spanish all year. Suddenly you notice that you've been laughing at the teacher's lame jokes in exactly the same way. And you realize that you're very fond of this person. In fact, you're friends.

Open Up

At some point in a new friendship, you may find yourself opening up—the fourth step of friendship. Perhaps you feel comfortable enough with your new friend to have the Big Talk, especially if you're girls. Suddenly you find yourself pouring your heart out or sharing something really important to you, and listening as your new friend shares his or her stuff with you. It's wonderful to connect with somebody new. You have a sense of mutual understanding. You may even feel like you've known each other forever.

Warning! Confiding is a vital part of friendship but it's really easy to get too carried away on your first Big Talks. Privacy is important, and it takes time to know if you can really trust somebody with your secrets. If it's really private, keep it to yourself until you know the person better. The friendship may become strong enough to carry deep confidences—or it may not. (There's more about sharing secrets in Chapter 4, "Friendship's Skills.")

Just Between Friends

Question: How do you know if this is going to be a true friend?

Answer: You don't. Let things develop naturally. Real friendships take time.

Try, Try Again

The fifth step to making a friend is knowing when to hang it up and let go gracefully. So you've sent out the good vibes. Maybe you've gotten past the initial getting-to-know-you phase and shared experiences and confidences in the Big Talk. And it just doesn't feel right, or there's no reciprocity—your calls don't get returned, you're dishing it out and nothing is coming back. If you keep making attempts with somebody and they just aren't responding, back down and try again with somebody else.

Sure, it's a disappointment. But it's time to muster up a deep breath, relax your shoulders, and move on. The world is full of lots of people. Not everybody can be a friend.

The Least You Need to Know

- Most people are shy about making new friends, but there are ways you can overcome your shyness.
- Friends don't just show up, it's up to you to make them.
- Increase your contact with new people.
- Open yourself up, be your real self, and people will respond.
- Not all potential friendships work out. Sometimes you can do something about it, and sometimes it's best to move on.

Chapter 3

Finding the Friend Within Yourself

In This Chapter

- The importance of being your own best friend
- Caring for yourself—body and soul
- Self-improvement, step by step
- Changing negative messages to positive affirmations

The first friend you need to make, before you make any other friends, is yourself. Why? Because it's almost impossible to make and keep friends when you're feeling lousy about yourself. In this chapter, we'll look at your relationship with yourself. Other friendships may come and go, but if you're a true friend to yourself, you'll always know who you can count on when times get tough—*you!*

It's not always easy to be a good friend to yourself. It means listening to yourself to find out what you need; expressing your needs; taking care of your mind, body, and emotions; drawing limits and saying yes and no; changing and growing; and improving your self-esteem and self-respect. These things take time. This chapter is just the start.

Being Your Own Best Friend

Hey, you don't need to just rely on others, you can be your own best friend (you can also be your own worst enemy, but we'll get into that later on in the chapter). Why would you want to be your own best friend? Two reasons:

- People will treat you the way you treat yourself.
- The way you treat yourself is generally the way you'll treat others.

Want to have good friends and be a good friend? Be a best friend to yourself, first. Best friends care about each other, stand up for each other, and look after each other. You can—and should—do that for yourself, too. Friends can't satisfy every need. They aren't always going to be there for you. You, however, can always be there for yourself.

A Friendly Reminder

Being your own best friend doesn't mean being your *only* friend. We all need friends.

Give Yourself a Break!

What's getting in the way of a great friendship with yourself? Probably your self-criticism working overtime. There's a big difference between seeing your faults and working to change them (a positive thing), and picking yourself to death over your real or perceived failings (a negative thing). We live in a critical world, and it's really easy to get hyper about what you look like or how you act. First of all, those things are not really who you are. More than that, though, I bet you don't look near as horrible as you imagine, and that nobody judges your social clumsiness as harshly as you do. Seeing yourself honestly is different from examining yourself under a microscope.

True-Life Friends

"Don't be so hard on yourself. You might not see what others see in you, the things that make you special."

—Sopheary, age 18

Practice Self-Respect, Gain Self-Esteem

All of the exercises in this book can help you improve your self-esteem, but the best thing by far for raising self-esteem is to treat yourself with respect. Make a commitment to treat yourself with respect. When you catch yourself putting yourself down (whether you're alone or with friends), STOP! Remind yourself that you are a great person who has a lot to offer!

Let Yourself Be Yourself

Being a friend to yourself means letting yourself be yourself. Honor your own feelings, tastes, joys, and dislikes. They're part of what makes you *you*. Be authentic. People respond best to real people.

True-Life Friends

"I think the key is not to try to be someone that you're not, but relax and go with the flow. Don't be scared to call people, and hang out with a wide variety of people, so you really get a feel for what you look for in a friend."

—Alicia, age 18

Learn to Like Being Alone

Some people are scared of spending time alone. We're not used to it in our culture. From daycare to school to afterschool activities, we're usually in a group. Even kids who come home after school to an empty house usually don't spend their time *really* alone: They immerse themselves in a serious relationship with Lara Croft or Tetris, or listen to music or spend the time talking on the phone ... anything to keep them from spending time alone with their brain.

I'm not saying that it's bad to be entertained. (It's fun!) The problem with relying too much on entertainment comes when you aren't comfortable being by yourself, you don't really like yourself, or you don't really know yourself.

Know Yourself

In order to like who you are, you have to *know* who you are. Try answering the following questions. Simply considering the questions (notice how they make you feel, too) should teach you a lot about yourself:

1. What are my favorite foods?
2. What are my favorite activities?
3. What kind of clothes do I like? What do my clothes say about who I am?
4. If I could go anywhere in the world I wanted to go right now, where would it be? Why?
5. How would my best friend describe me?
6. What do I want more than anything else in the world?
7. What's more important to me, love or money?
8. What are my passions and goals?

Well? Did you learn anything new about yourself?

Be Kind to Yourself

Friends do nice things for friends, so, as your own friend, you need to follow suit. Give yourself a break. If you've had an especially hard day or week, treat yourself to some special perks. Here are some ideas:

- Take yourself out for lunch or to a movie.
- Pack a picnic and eat in the park.
- Schedule a night of self-pampering (bath, facial, manicure, etc.).
- Buy a book or CD you've been craving.

Be Befriend-able

The best path to friendship is to be a fascinating, warm person. Focus on yourself—your health, your happiness, your interests—and you'll become more magnetic every day. People will be attracted to you. And don't worry about appearing stuck up—paying attention to your needs is not the same as being stuck on yourself.

Take Care of Your Body

Hey, you only get one body in this lifetime—treat it with respect! Being kind to your body means eating well, exercising, getting enough rest, keeping yourself clean, and putting on clothes that make you feel great.

What you eat has a direct relationship to how you feel. Every meal gives you choices. Keep making the healthier choices, and you'll soon feel better about yourself. Here are a few quick tips for a good diet:

- Educate yourself about nutrition.
- Balance your diet and eat a variety of foods.
- Fresh fruits and vegetables are best!
- Eat closer to the earth. That means that the less processed a food is, the better it is for you. A baked potato is better for you than sliced, frozen, or deep-fried French fries, for example.
- If you need to lose weight, do it gradually by upping your exercise level and reducing your intake of junk food and saturated fats.

Moving your body feels good. Exercise releases endorphins that make you feel great. It ups your energy, helps you sleep, and tones your body so you look great, too. Here are some quick tips for getting more exercise in your life:

- **Choose action over inaction.** A little less TV and a little more walking adds up. Walk up and down the stairs. Stretch while you're on the phone. Park far away from the mall entrance and really walk around while you're inside!

- **Shop around for a form of exercise you like.** Competitive sports? Noncompetitive sports? Outside exercise? Working out at a gym? Taking a dance class? Exercise doesn't have to be boring because there are so many different ways to get exercise.

- **Go slow.** Don't plunge into exercise like you're jumping off a cliff. If you're significantly overweight or you've been very inactive, check with your doctor before starting an exercise program.

Take Care of Your Emotions

A good friend pays attention to how you feel. As your own friend, you're responsible for knowing what you feel and honoring those feelings. When you pay attention to what you're feeling (even when those feelings are painful), you'll be better able to know what you want, what you like, and what you believe in. Nobody expects you to know the answer (most people take a lifetime to find out) but it sure is something to start thinking about now.

Making a Change for the Better

Take a good hard look in the mirror. No, not the one on the wall—the one deep inside yourself. Do you like what you see? Okay, face it, you're not perfect. Nobody is! Perhaps you're too judgmental. Maybe you tend to whine or you're really needy. Maybe you're so peeved about being liked for your looks, your brains, or the way you can dunk a basketball that you have a hard time trusting when anybody approaches you. Do people see the real you? How can they, when you're so busy hiding behind an attitude?

If you want to make changes in yourself, it helps to break the process into steps:

1. Decide on the goal (make it something reachable).
2. Figure out the small steps to get there.
3. Take the steps (one at a time, please).
4. Celebrate your successes—the little ones and the big ones.

Just Between Friends

Any goals you set for improving yourself should have a time factor. Not too short, not too long, and not too rigid! Without a time factor, you're just not going to achieve your goal.

Replacing Negative Messages with Positive Affirmations

To truly be a good friend to yourself and to others, you have to feel comfortable enough to trust yourself and the people around you. Only then can you open yourself up to friendship. "Affirmations" are a way to say "yes" to yourself, to care for yourself, to make changes, and to be your own best friend.

It's been said, "You are your own worst enemy." Most of us got at least one unconscious negative message when we were little kids. These messages might have come from our family, our school, our friends, or the world in general. Because we were little kids, we believed them. Believing these negative messages gets in the way of changing, growing, and being better friends to ourselves.

Here's a list of negative messages. Which feel the most familiar? Choose three that you most identify with:

A. Your needs don't matter; everybody else comes first.

B. Be nice. Don't get too assertive.

C. Work hard. You're part of a team here. Who cares what you feel or who you really are?

D. Don't ask for any favors. It's a hard world and you're on your own.

E. Be perfect, don't blow it, don't make any mistakes.

F. Your happiness doesn't matter—the world isn't about you, you know.

G. The world is dangerous. Don't get too comfortable.

H. People can't be trusted. Don't be a sucker! Don't open yourself up.

I. You don't know anything. You'll fail. Don't trust your feelings.

Poisonous, negative messages run deep in all of us, but you can defeat them! Following are some positive messages to counteract the negative ones:

A. I am wanted and loved. I listen to and support myself.

B. I matter. I assert my needs.

C. I am worthwhile and accepted just as I am.

D. I am strong and can depend on myself.

E. I'm a good person with all of my flaws.

F. My happiness matters.

G. The world welcomes and cares for me.

H. I am open and relaxed and trusting.

I. My intuition is strong and sure.

A Friendly Reminder

Just because this exercise sounds hokey and embarrassing doesn't mean you shouldn't try it. Affirmations have great power to change us and to make us feel better about who we are.

Write down your positive affirmations on a piece of paper or in a special notebook. Look in the mirror and say them out loud three times every day for a week. Words have power. You don't have to believe these affirmations to say them. But if you keep at it, pretty soon you will start believing the words!

The Least You Need to Know

- Before you can be friends with anyone else, you have to be your own best friend.

- Being your own friend means acknowledging your feelings, listening to your needs, and treating yourself with respect.

- Changing yourself requires making achievable, step-by-step goals with a time element, and celebrating even small achievements.

- You can replace negative messages with positive affirmations.

Chapter **4**

Friendship's Skills

In This Chapter
- Ten commandments for wonderful friendships
- Tips for keeping your friendships mutual, respectful, and loyal
- The art of communicating with your buds
- When to keep secrets—and when not to
- Ways to have fun and appreciate each other

Friendship may come naturally, but to be a great friend—supportive, fun, interesting, and loyal—you need a variety of skills. Some come easy; some you'll probably have to work on. This chapter contains details on friendship's skills.

My Ten Commandments for Successful Friendships

In Chapter 1, "Friendship: The Incredible Bond," I talked about the six things friends do for each other: give companionship, stimulation, physical support, ego support, social comparison, plus intimacy and affection. So, as a friend, how do you give your friends these things? With a drum roll, I present my 10 friendship commandments:

1. Thou shalt commit thyself to the friendship.
2. Thou shalt keep it mutual.
3. Thou shalt respect your friend and thyself.
4. Thou shalt be loyal and trustworthy.
5. Thou shalt be a good communicator.
6. Thou shalt know when to keep a secret (and when to tell one).
7. Thou shalt not just dump and run—thou shalt have fun!
8. Thou shalt compare, but shalt not compete.
9. Thou shalt express thine appreciation.
10. Thou shalt keep thine expectations in line.

Let's take a closer look at each of these commandments, shall we?

Just Between Friends

You're not perfect! None of us are. Don't get all stressed out and think you need to be the perfect friend. These commandments are skills to continuously work on, not automatically expect from yourself.

Commit Yourself

No, I don't mean to a mental institution! Good friendship is a commitment. To be a good friend, you need to care about the friendship and be willing to work on it. (The fact that you're reading this book shows how committed to friendship you are!)

Keep It Mutual

A friendship has got to be somewhat even. You help each other with your homework—you're good in Spanish, she's got your back in

American History. You both share your experiences, and you both know how to listen.

Of course, things can't be exactly even all the time. You don't need to keep a score sheet. A good friendship can take some imbalance. If you're going through a crisis—whether it's a love life disaster, a family calamity, or just a hard time in general—you may take up more time and energy than your friend. In a good friendship, this is nothing to worry about. Things will flip around, and in a little while, you'll be the sympathetic listener.

A Friendly Reminder

Some friendships need to work on their rec-iprocity. Think about the number of times you ask for homework help without reciprocating, or how often your friend has spent the night without asking you to her house. Keep it mutual. You don't want to be a user, and you don't want to be used.

Show Some R-E-S-P-E-C-T

Friendships thrive on mutual respect. If your friend doesn't have your back, who does? I've got a basic rule about who I choose to be friends with: No flakes or sleazeballs allowed! My friends need to respect my beliefs and problems and take me seriously. They can't make fun of me about anything important. (If they want to tease me about how I rub my nose vigorously with the heel of my hand or never quite know how to say goodbye, that's another matter. They're my friends, they're allowed.) As your own best friend, you have the special job of respecting yourself and wanting the best for yourself. One of friendship's skills is drawing the line at bad behavior. You deserve respect, love, and a caring ear from your friend. If you're not getting these things, it's time to re-evaluate the friendship!

Be Loyal and Trustworthy

A good friend is loyal and trustworthy—it's really a requirement. Loyalty means that you're on your friend's side. No, the two of you don't always have to agree, but you should know that when the chips are down, your friend can rely on you to stand up for him, and vice versa. Remember the cry of the Three Musketeers: One for all and all for one! Good friends are bonded.

Friendship also absolutely requires mutual trust. If you can't trust your friend, he or she isn't really your friend. This means that if your friend says she's going to do something, she'd better have a good reason for *not* doing it. If your friend is running late for a meeting with you, you expect him to call and let you know. As a friend, you should do your best to show up on time, tell the truth (but not cruelly), and never steal your friend's guy or girl. And in return, you should expect the same from your friend.

True-Life Friends

"Having younger friends is always a blast because you can be immature and careless once again. You can return the favor to them by giving them your knowledgeable advice, having gone through the same things at their age. It's a wonderful cycle."

—Alicia, age 18

Be a Good Communicator

Talking and listening (and even writing—think e-mail and pen pals) form the root of many friendships. If you're not talking and listening well to each other, your friendship's probably going through a rough time.

Listening is an art. A lot of times people hear what they want to hear, not what's really being said. A good listener gives what's being said time to sink in without jumping to conclusions or giving advice.

True-Life Friends

"The most important thing about communication is hearing what *isn't* being said."

—Marcus, age 18

A good friend pays attention to what's going on with a friend.
Listen to more than your friend's words. Sometimes the way your
friend looks, her actions, and her general posture can tell you when
something's going really well—or really wrong. If you're tuned into
your friend, you'll probably know when she needs to cry on your
shoulder without her saying a word. (There are more tips on talking
and listening in Chapter 11, "Friendly and Unfriendly Fighting.")

A good friend also knows when to express her opinions and when
to listen and keep her mouth shut. Here's some advice for you: Go
light on the advice! When your friend is upset, when he's really
down on himself or somebody else, what's your instinct? To tell him
what he should do? Nix that! Advice works best if it's doled out in
tiny doses. As a friend, the best thing you can do is to listen. Most
of the time, your friend will appreciate you helping her work things
out on her own better than she'll appreciate getting your advice.

Psychotherapists use this approach all the time. Many believe that,
if you really have the support to toss around ideas and express your
feelings, you'll find that the answer to your problems lies within
yourself. Of course, tell your friend your opinions, but you're better
off skipping the phrases "You should ..." and "If I were you, I'd ..."
Try using the words "Consider ..." or "Think about ..." instead.

Know When to Keep Secrets

Secrets and being able to confide in your friends bond friendships,
and in many cases they're an essential part of them. A friend can
give you a different perspective on a problem or share hard times

with you. A friend can also tell you when you're full of it. Confiding in someone can be tricky, because it often involves telling secrets. Some secrets are pretty trivial, like the time you wore your Dad's favorite hat, stained it, and had to get it dry-cleaned before you sneaked it back into his closet. Others are a lot more important, as we'll see in a moment.

True-Life Friends

"I've always had trouble with secrecy in friendships because I tend to tell friends absolutely everything and then regret it later."

—Alicia, age 18

When your friend tells you a secret, she gives you her trust. As a true and loyal friend, it's your job to resist turning it into gossip (more on gossip in Chapter 10, "Crimes Against Friendship"). Hearing secrets is tougher than it seems, because you have the responsibility to keep them to yourself. Telling somebody's secrets has a nasty way of boomeranging back to you. Your rep is on the line, so respect your friend's confidence and keep your lip zipped.

On the flip side, though, sometimes you have an obligation to tell somebody's secret, even when you know letting it out will embarrass your friend or hurt his feelings, or even get him into trouble. I'm talking about dangerous secrets that might lead to physical, mental, or emotional harm for your friend or someone else if you don't tell. Here's the bottom line of when you absolutely need to tell:

- When you or someone you know is threatened or has been harmed or abused, either sexually, mentally, or physically.

- When you know that someone's actions will hurt that person or someone else.

You don't necessarily need to tell a parent (although your parents can be an excellent source of advice) but you do need to tell *somebody*—the school nurse, a trusted teacher, a coach, whoever you feel will take the problem seriously and help your friend get the advice and help he or she needs. If your friend confides that he sometimes feels so bad that he cuts his arms to let the bad feelings out, he needs more help than you can provide by just listening. Or if your best friend tells you she tried Ecstasy at a party, or is having unprotected sex with her boyfriend, she needs to know what might happen to her (and why her choices aren't so great). Chapter 12, "A Friend in Need," has lists of resources and hotlines where you can tell somebody about your friend's problem and begin getting your friend solid advice and help.

If your friend is threatening violence against himself or somebody else, you need to act immediately. Telling is always better than not telling (the increasing violence in U.S. high schools should be enough to convince you). Take threats seriously! You—and everybody else—will be glad that you did.

A Friendly Reminder

If you really want a secret to remain a secret, keep it to yourself (or tell a professional therapist). People are only human—they slip up, forget, and mess up. (Yes, even your wonderful friends!)

Don't Just Dump and Run—Have Fun!

A friendship isn't just for complaining, confiding, and using each other as a sounding board. Neither of you will have much fun if both of you whine and moan all the time! Make sure that you build fun, games, activities, and giggles into your friendships.

Make a list of all the things you and your friend like to do together. Make another list of things you would like to try together. Then schedule time to do these things! Your lists might look like this:

Things we like to do:

- Bake cookies and eat them.
- Listen to music.
- Go to the video store and hang out talking about cult movies with the cute videohead who works there.

New things we'd like to try:

- Make up a new recipe and have a bake-and-eat party.
- Hold a CD swap so we can exchange new tunes.
- Take a filmmaking class at the rec center.

Another way to have fun is to aim for the positive. Friends can reinforce each other's positive behavior but they can also reinforce the negative, and when that happens, things can go from bad to worse.

Tonya and Shanda were both concerned about their weight. As they grew closer, instead of dealing with their weight issues by taking positive steps together, they started pigging out together. The more weight they gained, the more depressed they got, and the less time they spent hanging out with other friends. Pretty soon they spent all their time together, eating and eating. By the end of the year, Tonya had gained 25 pounds and Shanda had gained over 30. Both girls were totally depressed and angry about the weight gain, and constantly put each other down. The friendship had dissolved, but they had nobody else to turn to.

A great friend tries to focus on the positive sides of the friendship. If Tonya and Shanda had been able to do this (and they may have needed some outside support), maybe they would have started working out together instead of spending every afternoon pigging out.

Compare, But Don't Compete

Friends are a good measuring device for your own life. It's great to compare yourself with your friends, but it's *not* okay to compete with them, unless it's in sports. A good friend doesn't try to prove that she's smarter than her friends. She doesn't seek more attention from the opposite sex, doesn't boast about being a better artist, doesn't gloat over being cuter, doesn't brag about getting better grades … you get the idea.

Express Your Appreciation!

No, you don't *need* to share your candy bar or long-term lend him that CD he's been craving (although it's a nice idea). Still, your friend needs to hear how special he is to you. As part of the ego boost of friendship, it's your job to let your friend know he's wonderful. Everybody likes to be appreciated. Your friend won't know how much you like him unless you tell or show him.

Just Between Friends

You can't be everything to a friend, nor should you be. Hey! He's got other friends, he's got family, he's got teachers, and he's got himself.

Keep Your Expectations Appropriate

One friend can't satisfy all your needs and desires, or do it all the time. Don't expect the same things from all your friends. Different people fill different roles in our lives. It's important to know what each friend can give you in terms of air time, helping hands, patience, and shared activities. When you rely too much on just one or two people, you may be asking too much.

So, too, you may find that your friend is getting too needy. Look at her life. Are you her only friend? Maybe she needs encouragement to make more. Lend her this book. Help her meet new friends. Being a good friend means being available for her physical and emotional needs. No, you aren't on call, and yes, you have other things going on in your life, but a good friend wants to be involved in her friends' life.

The Least You Need to Know

- Friendship is natural, but the skill set isn't always intuitive. You've got to do some work!

- Friendship's a mutual thing: mutual time, mutual respect, mutual caring.

- Clear communication is key to a good friendship, whether it's talking or listening.

- It's important to have fun with your friends! Stay positive!

- Don't expect more from the relationship than it can give you.

2

Friendship in All Forms

Friends come in all varieties, and each variety has its own pleasures and complications. In this part, we'll look at details, details, details. Chapter 5 is all about the best friend: making one, dealing with the complications of having one, and separating from your best friend when you've developed a chronic case of Joined-at-the-Hipitis. Chapter 6 is about cliques and friendship with more than one person at a time. In Chapter 7, you'll gain skills for maintaining friendships at a distance (through pen, paper, and the wonders of technology). Then, in Chapter 8, we'll get to that fascinating form of friendship known as opposite-sex friends.

Chapter 5

The Best Friend

In This Chapter

- Best friend—nice to have, but not a requirement
- Finding your best buddy—or buddies
- Dealing with too much togetherness
- Tips for coping with your best friend's new friend
- When best-friendships end

Seems like everybody has the dream of having a best friend—somebody to hang with, understand you, share secrets with, and always pick you when you have to pair up for team projects. Yet not everybody has a best friend, or even needs one! This chapter is about the truths, myths, and problems that come with having a best friend (because, while having a best friend is incredibly fulfilling, it also has its hassles).

Best Friend Not Required

Xena and Gabrielle. Dawson and Joey. Buffy and Willow. Tom Sawyer and Huck Finn. Does it sometimes seem like you're the only one without a best friend? You're not. Some statistics say that only one third of all kids in high school have a best friend. That means that in a class of 30 kids, only 10 will have best friends. And while having a best buddy is a nice idea, it doesn't guarantee happiness.

So why don't you have a best friend? It may be that you haven't met the right person to be best friends with, or you're spreading yourself around a crowd of friendly people (and there's nothing wrong with that), or you're trying to single out one person as your best friend when you actually have two or more close friends.

Just Between Friends

"Best" implies that you can only have one. Lots of people have more than one really close friend who they call a "best friend"—it's kind of a shorthand expression. If you want to be accurate, try talking about your friend as a "very, very, very good friend," or "couldn't-feel-much-closer" friend.

Bingo! You're My Best Buddy!

Maybe you're in the one third of teens who have a best friend. What does best-friendship feel like? If you go back to the school-yard at your old elementary school and hang out for a while, you'll probably hear little kids talking about best-friendship all the time: "If you give me your candy, I'll let you be my best friend ..." and, "You're not my best friend any more!" (Of course, they also say "Na na na na na ..." and pick their noses a lot.)

When you get older, best-friendship becomes much deeper and not so petty as when you were a little kid. Best-friendship has to do with true caring, respect, and trust. A best-friendship requires ...

- Real, deep loyalty and commitment.
- Acknowledgment from both people in the friendship that the friendship really matters.

If you're somebody's best friend, that's a big responsibility. Time to brush up on your friendship skills! (Review Chapter 4, "Friendship's Skills," for a brush-up course.)

Just Between Friends

Best-friendship is just regular friendship with the volume cranked.

When Is Tight Too Tight?

Are you and your best friend inseparable? Okay, you've been best friends since third grade. Your friend's mom is practically your mom; your brother teases your best friend like he teases you. You're always together, you always have each other, you can finish each other's sentences, you talk and think alike. Maybe the two of you are even referred to as a single unit, like Katy and Ayala, who kids call Katala—and they both answer.

"Those two are thick as thieves," you hear your grandma say as you and your best bud head to your bedroom for some homework and gossip time. Or your dad pulls you aside and suggests that you take up soccer to make new friends. "Not that I think Lee is a bad influence on you, but it's better to expand your horizons," he lectures. Not exactly a ringing endorsement of your best-friendship, is it? It's true that people can feel uncomfortable when you and a friend are so bonded. Milo and I were the "Gruesome Twosome" in high school. It's not that we looked alike (she's fair and I'm dark) but we were both kind of short and opinionated, and we were always together so people often associated us with each other. Years later, we still talk with the same intonation, finish each other's sentences, and laugh at the same memories. Of course, somewhere along the line we stopped being the "Gruesome Twosome" and just became very close friends.

A Friendly Reminder

Don't cling! The best way to nurture your best-friendship is to stay self-reliant, and this means having friends other than your best friend.

Joined at the Hip

Inseparable friendship serves a real purpose in the teen years. That's probably why people tend to pair up. Here are some of the advantages of having a best friend this tight:

- You know you're secure and cared for.
- You never have to be alone.
- You can learn from each other.
- It makes it easier to switch social groups. Since you're doing it as a unit, you appear less insecure.
- You can egg each other on to get braver and bolder and less shy.
- Nobody better mess with you because somebody's always got your back.
- If you have a crush on somebody, your friend can drop a hint, take a message, or arrange a rendezvous for you (and vice versa).

Yet, sometimes the joined-at-the-hip relationship can actually cause problems for the two friends:

- It's hard to maintain or build your own sense of identity when you're always with the same person. You can begin to feel swallowed up. You want to be known for your own self, not just a part of a partnership.
- You may rely too heavily on your friend for certain skills and not learn how to do them for yourself.

- It can be hard to branch out and meet new people.

- Whether or not you feel intimidating yourselves, a real tight friendship can be seen as a solid wall against the rest of the world.

- And if one of you does make a new friend (especially if it's a close new friend), the other friend will probably feel jealous and left out. It's only human.

True-Life Friends

"We were like Tweedledum and Tweedledee—it was cool, but it was also a little stuffy in there. We're still friends, though."

—Chris, age 14

Breaking Out Without Breaking It Up

What happens when one best friend is ready for other friendships, different activities, or just a change of scenery? In the case of me and my friend Milo, after two years of being the Johnson-Lutz twins, she'd had enough. She made new friends and then, when I got clingy and upset, she wrote me a long letter telling me I still mattered to her a lot but that she was tired of always hanging out with me. Yeah, it hurt. And she'll be the first to admit that it wasn't the best way to handle it. I didn't behave much better—I sulked! Then after a month or so of misery watching Milo giggle with her new pals, I separated myself and started hanging out with a new group of kids. Seeing me so involved with other friends, *she* started feeling left out.

Milo is still absolutely one of my best friends. We would have avoided a lot of misery, though, if we'd understood that what we were going through was a natural development. We really didn't need each other that much anymore! If we'd understood that, we might have known that there were better ways of handling it than sending accusatory letters and sulking.

Here are some tips if you start feeling like your best friend is always in your face:

- Move toward doing things together with a group of other people. Sports teams, dramatic shows, church groups … in all these situations, it's hard to pair off. You'll still be together, but you won't be exclusive. (On a team, for instance, you all work together towards getting better and winning!)

- Talk to your friend about how you feel. He may surprise you and tell you that he's been feeling a little stifled himself, or he may take it as a rejection, no matter how gently you phrase it. Make sure you reassure your friend how much you care about him.

- Change is hard, so do your best not to make any sudden changes. If you're joined at the hip one day and distant strangers the next, your pal is going to feel hurt and cut off. That's not a good way to show your caring.

A Friendly Reminder

Making new friends will affect how much time you can spend with your best bud. But never, ever break a date with your best friend for a new friend!

When Others Step In

Whether you're best friends for life or just pals, things can get sticky when another person steps in. It's natural to feel jealous of your best friend's new friendship and the time he spends with that person. If you or your best friend has a new friend, remember that he wouldn't be your best friend if he didn't care for you—a lot. Your friendship is not in danger just because he's met somebody new.

Okay, let's say you're fine with the thought of your best friend having other friends. But how do you cope if you can't stand her new friend? Keep these tips in mind:

- You don't have to like your best friend's new friend—just as she doesn't have to like your new friend. It's nice if it happens, but if it doesn't, that doesn't say anything bad about any of you. Not everybody likes each other!

- Never badmouth your best friend's other friend. It won't do anything but make your best friend mad and uncomfortable. You can't convince your best friend that her new friend is a loser, so don't even try. Concentrate on being a great friend to your friend. If her new friend is bad news, she'll figure it out on her own.

- Make an effort to get to know the new person. You may find you really like her, even though you were prepared to hate her for "taking away" your best friend. Give her a chance!

A Friendly Reminder

You can't force best-friendship. That's why it's better to think of people as "close friends" rather than "best friends."

The End of the Line

Sad to say, but some best-friendships don't last. Maybe you and your best friend have a major blowout that alters your feelings for each other, or you just drift apart gradually. No matter how it occurs, breaking up with your best friend can be just as hard or harder than breaking up with a boyfriend or girlfriend—complete with a formal discussion, tears, storming out, accusatory letters, or flaming e-mails. There's more about the end of friendships in Chapter 13, "Friendship's End," but for now, if your best-friendship is ending, keep the following in mind:

- Don't feel guilty. Best friends often stop being best friends and sometimes they stop being friends completely.

- Moving from best friends to just regular friends can be a slow, natural process. Over time, you get interested in different things and people and you just don't have as much in common any more. This transition becomes hard when one of you resists. Talk to each other about what's happening.

- Best-friendships—like all friendships—have a natural life span. It's the rare (and lucky) ones that last a lifetime.

- Don't let anyone tell you, "Oh, cheer up, it's just a friend. It's not like it's a relationship or anything." If you feel bad, go ahead and cry! You'll feel better if you acknowledge how much it hurts to lose a best friend.

The Least You Need to Know

- If you don't have a best friend, you're not alone—only one third of all kids in high school have a best friend.

- A good way to nurture your best-friendship is to have friends other than your best friend.

- Inseparable friendships sometimes lead to over-reliance and a sense of being stifled.

- Never betray your best friend for a new friend!

- All friendships—even best-friendships—have a natural life span. Only rarely do they last a lifetime.

Life in the Group of Friends

In This Chapter

- The fun and confusion of group friendship
- Clique city! All you ever need to know
- The real rub on popularity
- About labels and limits

Up until now we've been talking about one-on-one friendship; "just me and my bud" friendship, the two of you together. Now it's time to branch out. This chapter is about friendship with more than one person at a time—friendships in groups and cliques. Life in the group means more friends to watch your back, more people cheering you on as you round third base and head for home, and more pals supporting you if you decide to run for president of your class.

It's Different in a Group!

Friendship in groups is similar to friendship one-on-one in a lot of ways. It's about having fun together as a group, supporting each other, stimulating each other, boosting your ego, and all the other elements of friendship (go back to Chapter 1, "Friendship: The

Incredible Bond," for a review). Friendship in groups provides *more* of a social mirror and, generally, *less* intimacy than friendship one-on-one does.

Friendship in a group is not only fun, it's a great way to learn more about socializing. The dynamics of having to get along with a bunch of people really sharpens your social skills. Friendships also tend to become more complicated when there's more than two of you together. (Think of all the complications that arise every week on the TV show *Friends!*) What kinds of complications? Let's take a look.

Decisions Take Longer

The more people who have to be considered for every decision, the longer making that decision takes. Maybe that's why you always end up ordering a large pepperoni and a large vegetarian pizza—they're the only two the majority can agree on. And maybe that's why you all end up hanging out in front of the TV, even though you say you're going to all go to the movies this time. Again.

Jealousy Strikes!

Jealousy and frustration can also happen in a group of friends. You're worried that your buds all seem to get the joke and you don't, Jakob spends more time with Lance than he does with Mike and you, Theo and Lamarr ride to school on their scooters while you and Devonte are stuck on foot. It's not fair. When you're measuring yourself against a whole group of buds, your own failings seem to stand out.

True-Life Friends

"If you ever have three really good friends, one always seems to be left out, and I never know how to fix that. So I say stick to an even number of friends to be close to."

—Alicia, age 18

Clique City!

Love them or hate them, but we can't talk about groups of friends without talking about cliques. There are cliques in just about every culture in the world. (Sometimes they're called political parties or professional organizations or High Society.) A clique is a group of people, made up of good friends, close friends, best friends, and other friends, that has an exclusive element to it.

Teens generally feel one of two ways about cliques:

- They're in one, so they feel fine about cliques.
- They're not in one, and they feel left out, unaccepted, or, worst of all, unacceptable.

Not just anybody can join a particular clique. Often, the "rules" about who can join are unspoken (even the clique's members might not understand them all). The rules might be based on what you look like, what church your family goes to, the clothes you wear, the types of classes you like, your grades, a shared appreciation of comic books, the kind of music you listen to, or anything at all.

A Friendly Reminder

It's the exclusive element that makes cliques so dangerous. Social isolation and rejection can lead to teen depression, and in extreme situations (as you know so well from the violence happening in high schools), self-injury or violence toward others.

Clique = Closed

Since a clique is exclusive by definition, here's my advice: Don't waste your time trying to be accepted by one. The straight-on approach rarely works anyway. Here are some other things to think about:

- If you think one of the people in the clique seems interesting, concentrate on making friends with that person separately from clique activities. (Go back to Chapter 2, "How to Make a Friend," to brush up on your friend-making skills.)

- Focus on being friends with yourself (go back to Chapter 3, "Finding the Friend Within Yourself," to brush up on the details). If you become as cool and interesting as you can by taking care of yourself, trying new activities, learning new things, and being friendly, clique members might approach you. Then you can decide if you want to be part of the group (you may be too cool and interesting for them, anyway!).

- If the people in the clique that you're interested in are really judgmental and turn up their noses at letting "just anyone" join, forget them. Do you really want to be associated with such a superficial group? Focus on making a few good friends from a variety of social scenes. (To tell you the truth, members of very exclusive cliques often feel stuck with their limited social circle.)

A Friendly Reminder

If you're in a clique and they don't like your new friend, it's time to reassess the situation. You can't force people to like each other, and nobody should put pressure on you to stop liking somebody, either. Stand up for your new friend. If the group doesn't lay off, ask yourself what's more important to you: being part of the clique or your new friendship.

Alone in the Crowd

On top of everything else about cliques, being accepted by one doesn't guarantee social happiness. By no means! A person can be a member of a crowd, yet not have any friends. Man, can that feel lonely. If you're a lonely face in the crowd, here are a couple of comments for you:

- Work on making friends with somebody in your group to hang out with away from the rest of the crowd. If you can bond with one nice person, you'll feel better.

- Know that you have a total leg-up on the situation by already being a member of the clique. Making friends with another member may not be as difficult as you think. After all, you already have something in common—you hang out with the same people, at the same places, and have shared experiences.

- If you really feel alone and you're unsuccessful at making friends with anybody, reconsider the kids. Maybe they're jerks. Or maybe you really don't have that much in common with them, and it's time to find another crowd or just concentrate on making one or two good friends.

True-Life Friends

"Cliques and groups are part of everyday life. You might not even know that you're in one yourself. Just beware of that and don't discriminate. Be kind to everyone."

—Sopheary, age 18

The Truth About Popularity

We spend a lot of time fretting about popularity. There's even a TV show called *Popular* that puts the spotlight on these issues. "Am I popular?" "So and so is more popular than me!" "If I join the basketball team, maybe I'll be more popular ..." We spend so much time thinking and stressing over something that is, frankly, not worth worrying about at all. Popularity means being widely liked, and it's overrated.

True-Life Friends

"Real-life high school is nothing at all like in the movies. Of course there's the famous 'popular crowd' and the 'nerds' and so on, but in real life, it's the smart kids who are cool and the populars know that."

—Liliana, age 18

What's wrong with popularity? Only that you have to work so hard at it. You have to know what's cool, buy what's cool, do what's cool ... that's a lot of pressure (and time and energy). Consider these statements about popularity:

- Popularity is unpredictable and fickle. You might be popular for a week and then someone else may take your place.

- Having friends is related to having good self-esteem, but being popular is not. A lot of people who identify themselves as popular actually don't have good self-esteem.

- You might be popular and well-liked by a group yet not have a single close friend.

- You might not be wildly popular but be very successful at friendship.

- Popularity has little or no relationship to your inner strength, your wonderful qualities, your ethics and integrity, and your ability to succeed in life.

A Label Is a Limit

We all wear labels in life (and not just on our clothing). Here are some of the labels we might wear in middle school and high school: artist, street, jock, granola, brain, stuck-up, suck-up, babe, dawg, richie, preppie, stoner, punk, hippie ....

And here's a sample of some of the labels we might wear in life: female, male, black, white, gay, straight, American, Chinese, New Yorker, Californian, construction worker, white-collar worker, rich, poor, sexy, ugly, boring, fascinating, socialite, sociopath, Republican, Democrat, parent, grandparent, environmentalist, old, young, ex-con, soccer Mom, writer, banker, Nobel-Prize winner ... the list is endless.

A Friendly Reminder

Don't feel sorry for kids who have friends but who aren't part of the "popular" crowd. They're fine. It's the kids who don't have any friends at all who are the ones in social trouble.

Labels tell something about us quickly, but labels can never tell the whole truth about a person. They limit our self-image of who we are or can become. (How many labels in the lists above fit you?) People also make assumptions about who you are based on the social group you hang out with—but this label doesn't tell the whole story, either. Why can't you be in more than one group at a time? You can, and probably are. I'm part of the ice skating group at my local ice rink. I meet with a bunch of other writers once a month. I have a group of friends from high school that I still keep in touch with.

Having more than one group of friends is a healthy thing. It's an opportunity to explore all the various sides of yourself, because no one group can represent all of who you are. Group identity can help you identify who you really are—but don't let group friendship limit you.

The Least You Need to Know

- Group friendship provides more of a social mirror and less intimacy than one-on-one friendship does.

- A clique is a "closed" group; its exclusivity is part of what makes it a clique.

- Popularity is overrated, and takes a lot of time and pressure to maintain.

- You are not defined by any one group you belong to.

Chapter 7

Long-Distance and Virtual Friendships

In This Chapter

- Long-distance friendship techniques
- Want to be my pen pal?
- A few words about the telephone
- Tips on using e-mail correctly—and a few scary realities
- Life in the chatroom
- What your "virtual friends" can—and can't—give you

Once upon a time, before the Internet, the telephone, or even the post office, a friend was somebody you spent time with in the same room (or cave). Now, people across the globe are friends with each other, and although they might never meet, they share elements of their lives in a meaningful way. Friends in real life share intimacies over the Internet because it's easier to open up on life. Ah, technology!

This chapter is about long-distance and virtual friendships, whether it's with your chatroom buddy, a friend who's moved away, or a teen who lives in another hemisphere.

Friends You Don't (or Rarely) See

Long-distance friendships rarely have the intensity of day-to-day friendships. Without the physical presence of your friend, you're free to concentrate on ideas and emotions. On the other hand, you don't have the reality of a friend in daily life. These friendships are the "light" version. You can always log off, unplug, and ignore. Long-distance friendship has its benefits and its pitfalls. We'll take a look at both.

A Friendly Reminder

When long-distance and telephone friendships take up more time and energy than "real" friendships, something is out of balance. We all need real, in-person friends!

The Old-Fashioned Pen Pal

Once upon a time (again), people had a fine tradition of exchanging letters with each other. Many people still enjoy being pen pals with other people all over the globe. With pen pals, weeks can go by between communications. People who love being pen pals tend to appreciate this time lag; it means they have time to carefully craft each letter. They also like having mementos—actual letters to reread in the tub, tuck into their underwear drawer, and so on. These days, pen pals have largely turned into e-mail and chatroom pals. (There's more about e-mail and chatrooms coming up later in this chapter.)

The Telephone Lifeline

The telephone adds a lot to teen friendships, although it can also lead to problems, misunderstandings, and a heck of a big phone bill, especially if your friend lives far away. Telephone conversations play a big part in long-distance friendships; the telephone provides an "immediate" way to keep in touch.

Just Between Friends

The telephone—who uses it, how much it's used, and who pays the bill—can be a major source of conflict between teens and their parents. If you use the phone a lot (and what teen doesn't!) and you have a job, think about contributing a few bucks toward the monthly bill (ideally, before your parents ask!).

Many teens spend hours a day on the phone with friends. Pay attention to your own energy level. If you're tired and cranky because it's the end of the day, you might be giving yourself a message about what you really need—space and time alone! Time to get off the phone.

Cell phones (short for cellular phones) are a great invention. They're also an expensive invention. Limit the number of calls you make to your friend's cell phone, especially if you're calling from a land line (mobile-to-mobile might be free, depending on your friend's plan). Those minutes count! Be hyper-aware of your use and abuse of cell phone time. Cell phones shouldn't be used for general gossip and chatting. It's easy to lose track of the number of minutes you're racking up, and those calls can be expensive. In general, consider cell phones an advanced paging system and keep your conversations short, short, short.

E-Mail Tips

E-mail (short for electronic mail) has brought back writing as a popular communication form. Although e-mail is still a fairly new invention, with customs and social rules still evolving, it's been around long enough to get a lot of people in trouble and damage a lot of friendships. How does this happen? Through using it improperly. E-mail lends itself, unfortunately, to misunderstandings. To be the best e-mail buddy on the planet, it's vital to understand a few facts about how e-mail should and shouldn't be used.

> ## A Friendly Reminder
>
> Online friendships are simply a different breed of friendship. They are not a substitute for the "real" thing.

E-Mail Is Public Mail

Think your e-mail is private? Think again. People can access the commercial server you use. If you go through a school, the school administration has access to it; and if you go through a company (say, you're using your dad's account), that company has access to it. In lawsuits and court cases, it's not unusual for evidence found on computer hard drives and in e-mail records to be used in the courtroom.

And did you know that e-mail can be forwarded to anybody else without you knowing it and without your permission? There are new programs that can "tag" e-mail and track it to see where it goes (although those programs are not infallible or widely used). It's also easy to copy and paste incriminating text into another program's document, copy and paste it back into the e-mail program, and voilà—a "clean" forwarded e-mail!

All this means one thing: E-mail may feel private when it's just you and your friend on the other end, but it's not!

E-Mail Is Forever

The joy of e-mail is its speed. The horror of e-mail is … well, its speed. One slip of the finger and the nasty words, gushy sentiments, or shared gossip you write goes out into the land of bits and bytes and it's out of your control forever. You can't take it back!

E-Mail Has No Sense of Humor

E-mail is flat, it's on a screen, it has no voice. As a result, it's really hard to tell when the e-mailer is being funny, sarcastic, or just plain rude. (That's why they invented emoticons—those little smiley faces or other expressions you can insert into your e-mails.)

With e-mail, you have to work harder to make yourself understood than you do when talking with your friends either on the phone or in person. Run into trouble? E-mail misunderstanding and hurt feelings? Hint: Don't flame! Pick up the phone and clarify the problem.

True-Life Friends

"E-mail is an awesome way to keep in contact. Trust me, being a college student away from friends and family is hard, and getting a little letter or note does wonders!"

—Sopheary, age 18

E-Mail Can Be Addictive

You've spent all day together at school, and now you're home exchanging e-mails with your friends! What's up with that? Sure, e-mail is great for exchanging information, and not too shabby for getting to know new friends. Watch out though, that your e-mail friendship doesn't take over spending "real" time with each other. It's way too easy to get so deeply involved in your computer that you lose track of time. Got those dark circles under your eyes, that pasty look from never seeing the sun? Try turning the computer OFF!

E-Mail Has Etiquette

Like any form of communication, there are polite ways and impolite ways to use e-mail. Here are a few tips:

- All caps is like shouting. Don't put your messages in all caps, it's rude!

- Using threads (pieces of the other person's message) when you reply is great, but just pick out the important pieces instead of constantly sending the entire message back and forth.

- Never forward somebody's message without that person's permission.

- Give your e-mail a quick read before you send it. Wading through a sea of typos and poor grammar is distracting for your reader and makes you look bad.

- Think twice before blasting your friend with an angry e-mail. Remember, once you've sent it, you can't take it back. Give yourself time to cool off; you may feel differently tomorrow. If you're upset with your friend about something, it's better to talk it out in person or on the phone.

- Enough with the endlessly recycled jokes and petitions, okay? Don't bog down your friends with a steady stream of junk e-mails.

Chatrooms and Instant Messaging

The Internet is home to thousands of chatrooms, sites where you can chat 24/7 with people from all over the world. Lots of these sites cater to teens (or creeps *pretending* to be teens). Chatrooms are often organized around a theme or interest, like music or sports. No matter what you're into, chances are a number of other people are, too, and would love to chat with you about it.

Chats are generally public forums with numerous people chatting (typing in) comments at the same time. It takes a while to get used to the rhythm of chatting. Try it a few times and you'll soon catch on. If you're trying to get the flavor or style of a particular chatroom, hang out for a while as a lurker. Figure out what's going on before you join in. Most chats have the option of going to a private virtual "room" to chat in private with somebody. This might be somebody you've just met, or it might be somebody you have an ongoing online relationship with.

True-Life Friends

"If you're chatting with someone you don't know, don't give them any personal information like your home address. Your first name is fine unless you have a really unique first name. You never know what type of freak is on the other end and you don't want a stalker."

—Malancha, age 18

Instant Messaging is another option. With Instant Messaging technology, you can "chat" in real time with a specific person, but you have to set it up ahead of time. This is a great option for long-distance friends or relationships, as well as for getting to know your "real" friends better. It's sometimes easier to open up with somebody when you're not face to face.

Virtual Friendship vs. Real Friends

Way back in Chapter 1, "Friendship: The Incredible Bond," I told you about the six things that friendship provides: companionship, stimulation, physical support, ego support, social comparison, and intimacy/affection. "Virtual friends"—people you are pals with but have never met face to face, such as chatroom buddies, e-mail acquaintances, or pen pals—provide some, but not all, of these elements of friendship. Let's see how they stack up:

- **Companionship.** Check! If you're feeling lonely or alone, your virtual pals can help. At midnight, when you're sleepless in Seattle, it's morning in Paris. Your pal is wide awake and online with you telling you about her delightfully flaky croissant and *chocolat chaud*.

- **Stimulation.** Check! What better way to learn about people from different places and cultures than from people of different places and cultures?

- **Physical support.** Nope. Your virtual buddies aren't physically available to help you do your geometry homework or paint your toenails.

Just Between Friends

Sharing intimate secrets with strangers sometimes feels easier than sharing them with people you know.

- **Ego support.** Check! You can get your ego boosted online. You can even get your alter ego's ego boosted online; chatrooms and e-mail lists lend themselves to invented lives, looks, and personalities. Of course, that can be a dangerous thing, as we'll see in just a moment.

- **Social comparison.** Hmmm. Not really. Social comparison happens in groups of friends who know each other. You learn about yourself and where you fit in socially by looking at your friends. In virtual friendships, there really is no group (other than the e-mail discussion group you're all members of). You don't get a sense of where you fit in your society the same way you do in "real" life.

- **Intimacy/affection.** Emotional intimacy, sometimes; affection, not a chance. Your screen is cold, hard, and made of glass. Your keyboard can't hug you when you're down. You are not in the same room with your virtual buddies. There's no human touch. You need "real" friends for this aspect of friendship.

Keep Your Boundaries Distinct

For your own safety—and I'm talking both emotional and physical safety now—it's vital to keep your virtual friends virtual. Horror stories abound about people who've lied about their ages, sexes, and criminal records and lured teens to meet them in person, or at least to give out personal information.

A Friendly Reminder

If you're feeling at all weird about somebody you've met online, trust that feeling. Cut off contact, change your screen name, and let somebody know about it: your parents, a trusted teacher, or a friend. Don't be a victim!

Long-Distance Joy

Making, keeping, and maintaining friendship over wires and through the mail can enhance your life tremendously. It feels great to sense the world as a friendly place, filled with caring people. If you find yourself spending more time with your virtual friends than your real friends, though, it's time to pull back and rebalance. It's all a matter of balance!

The Least You Need to Know

- Long-distance and virtual friendships are "friendship light." You can always log off, turn off, or ignore.

- The advantage of old-fashioned pen pals is the time lag. No risk of flaming here!

- The telephone can be a wonderful way to maintain friendships. Watch those minutes, though, they add up!

- E-mail is public and can damage friendships when used improperly.

- As long as you're wise about using them, chatrooms can provide countless sources of information, support, and fun.

- Keep your boundaries distinct and your personal information private.

Chapter 8

Guys and Girls as Friends

In This Chapter

- The advantages of having friends of the opposite sex
- The different ways guys and girls communicate
- When people misunderstand the friendship
- When you can't be just friends
- Getting along with your friend's "significant other"

When you were in grade school, chances are girls hung out with girls and boys hung out with boys. You probably didn't like the same things and you didn't mix any more than you had to. But times have changed, people grow up, and for teens, the days of cooties are over.

If you're a young teen, you're probably hanging out with the opposite sex for the first time since preschool. There's probably a lot of good-natured teasing going on. There may be some hooking up. For the most part, though, there's a lot of checking out the opposite sex and trying on friendships and relationships to see what feels comfortable. If you're an older teen, hanging out with both sexes probably feels more natural. Older teens tend to incorporate both guys and girls in groups. But what about real *friendship* between guys and girls? That's the focus of this chapter.

Guys and Girls as Friends

Oh, there are so many advantages to having a friend of the opposite sex! A guy or girl can give you insight into the way their sex does things, thinks about things, and communicates. If you're a girl with a guy friend, it's like having an "in" on how guys see things—and vice versa. Here are a few other advantages of friendship with the opposite sex:

- There's likely to be less comparison, competition, jealousy, fighting, and tension than in a same-sex friendship.

- It can feel comfortable and reliable, like the brother or sister you *wish* you had.

- It can be a safe place to explore intimacy without sexuality.

True-Life Friends

"I totally love Renee but not in a romantic way. I feel totally comfortable around her, I mean, she sees my silly side and that's rare. But romance? No way. We just don't have that ... sizzle."

–David, age 15

"A Chance to Be Free"

Bill always hung out with girls as well as with guys; his best friend in high school was a girl named Marlene. With her and his other female friends he felt free to giggle and show his sensitive side, be a fool, cry, and play, without thinking about how old he was. With his guy friends he always felt the pressure to be macho and talk "guy stuff." Bill loved what he calls "girl energy."

His friendships with girls were also a place to play around with sexual innuendo without having it be serious. His friends could tease him about girls who liked him and it was fun. Bill, like many other teens, found his friendships with members of the opposite sex a place to relax.

True-Life Friends

"With my friends who are girls I don't have to put on airs, I can just be me."

–Bill, age 17

Comfort and Understanding

Friendships with people of the opposite sex can also provide great comfort and understanding after a love relationship ends. Alicia and her friend Marcus got close when they were both out of difficult relationships and needed the advice and comfort of the opposite sex without the tension of a romance. Hanging out together helped each of them get over the pain of breaking up with others. They even dated briefly, but stopped when they realized that their romantic relationship was jeopardizing their friendship. (For more on friendship turning into romance into romance, see Chapter 9, "Friendship and Romance.")

The Different Ways Girls and Guys Communicate

Once you start hanging out with teens of the opposite sex, you'll start to notice differences in how they communicate, specifically in how they talk and how they listen. At times you might feel as though you speak different languages! The fact is, studies have shown that guys and girls really *do* have different ways of communicating:

- Guys tend to be direct and say what they think. They lay it on the line. They show their support by taking a problem-solving approach to listening—if you come to a guy with a problem, he's likely to tell you just how to solve it. At times, though, guys can be noncommunicative and need their space.

- Girls tend to use talk to build and maintain friendships and relationships, express support through listening, and let others know they care about what's being said. Girls may also say what they think you want to hear, or sugarcoat the truth to spare a friend's feelings.

True-Life Friends

"My friend Joshua is so quiet unless he has something to *say*, and I'm such a chatterbox; and then I'm not sure he's listening so I just get louder. I just don't believe in bottling it up inside."

–Selena, age 14

You Don't Have to Get Romantic

In classic Hollywood movies, there's only one real plot where members of the opposite sex are concerned: Boy meets girl, boy loses girl, boy gets girl, boy and girl live happily ever after. There aren't a lot of movies where boy and girl meet and become best buds. But think about it: When you assume that guys and girls can only be romantic partners, you're missing out on friendship with half the human race! Yes, you can be friends with a member of the opposite sex without romance. And no, this kind of friendship is not just a second-rate substitute for a first-rate relationship. Good friends don't always make good romantic partners. Value what you have.

When They Think You're Involved and You're Not!

Just because you and your friend are clear that the two of you are just friends doesn't mean the rest of the world will be. People tend to assume that if you're hanging with somebody of the opposite sex, you're involved with that person.

Malancha had a good guy friend. They enjoyed talking with each other and enjoyed each other's company, but they were not involved romantically. Malancha's friend had a girlfriend who felt very threatened by Malancha, so much so that she pulled her boyfriend away whenever she saw him and Malancha having a conversation.

Everybody at school assumed Malancha and her guy friend were going out, or that they wanted to. Rumors started flying about Malancha liking him, and him liking her, and eventually even they started to believe the rumors. "It was sometimes hard to say or act in a certain way without it being interpreted in the wrong way," Malancha says. With both of them confused and upset, the friendship dissolved. "I wish I was more honest with him in the beginning, and I wish I hadn't let his girlfriend, our friends, our families, or our classmates get in the way, because I lost a pretty good friend," Malancha says regretfully. Malancha's story had a sad ending because she and her friend weren't clear on how to handle the pressures.

It's really nobody else's business who you choose to spend time with. If the friendship is important to you, stand up for it! But if it bothers you that your friendship with somebody of the opposite sex is misunderstood, here are some tips:

- Make it very clear verbally both to each other and to other people about where the two of you stand with each other.

- If your opposite-sex friend is in a relationship, be aware that your friend's partner might feel threatened by you. Try getting to know the person. Once he or she sees that you're not a threat, the tension will probably dissolve. (There's more on this a little later in the chapter.)

- If your friend is reluctant to let you meet his or her partner, your little bunny ears should perk up because something else is going on. Is your friend hiding something? Lying about something? Harboring secret fantasies about *you?* It's time for a little heart-to-heart to find out what's up.

- You and your friend might agree to spend more time in groups and less time alone with each other.

Just Between Friends

When it comes to friendship, openness and honesty are always the best policies. Say what you mean and express what you feel.

Help! I Look "Taken"

Your friendship with a person of the opposite sex might, if misunderstood, cramp your style in the love department and scare away people who are interested in getting to know you romantically. If this is a concern for you or you're running into problems with your love life because of your opposite-sex friends, consider these ideas and tips:

- Are you, in fact, emotionally available? You may not want or need a boyfriend or girlfriend right now. You might be getting your intimacy needs met through friendship.

- It's easy to let people know you aren't "taken" if you know them or they go to your school—just pass it along through the grapevine.

- It can bode well for a potential love interest to stay back— way back—because he or she thinks you're "taken." Nice people don't want to move in on somebody else's partner.

- If people consistently get the wrong idea about you and your pal, you need to look at why. Are you being exclusive? Giggling in corners? Being physically affectionate? There's nothing wrong with any of these things. You're just going to need to work a little harder to set the record straight.

- Occasionally, you might *want* to "look taken." It's great to have an opposite-sex friend to step in and fill the role of sweetheart. It's a no-muss, no-fuss way to discourage that undesirable person who's hitting on you, for instance. Just make sure you're not hurting feelings when you do it.

True-Life Friends

"My friend Joanie and I are always hugging and holding hands. People think we're lesbians. We don't happen to be, we're just affectionate. In other cultures, even guys put their arms around each other!"

—Tracie, age 13

When You Just Can't Be Friends

While the idea of being friends with members of the opposite sex might sound great, sometimes it doesn't work. Many people have an easy time making and keeping friends of the opposite sex. For others, romantic feelings too often get in the way.

Lucky was in love with her best male friend for three years, and he was in love with her, too, but neither of them knew how to approach the relationship safely. They were afraid of ruining their friendship, and also afraid of not taking the chance to be together. Eventually Lucky realized she couldn't handle not being romantic with her friend, and needed to separate herself from him. He didn't know what he had done wrong and why she was so distant. The friendship was strained, and eventually ended. Both were terribly hurt.

True-Life Friends

"I think it's really hard to be so close without getting intimate or feeling like you want to be more than just friends with that person."

—Lucky, age 19

Ask yourself: Is there a romantic component to the friendship and you're just not admitting it? If the answer is yes, then you're in a dishonest and potentially heartbreaking situation, unless it's clear both of you feel the same way. There's more on the journey from friendship to romance and back again in Chapter 9.

A Friendly Reminder

It may be tempting to fool around sexually with your friend. You like this person, you care about him or her, you're close ... and after all, you've got hormones. DANGER! DANGER! FRIEND-SHIP RISK ALERT! Proceed with extreme caution (if at all).

Getting Along with Your Friend's "Significant Other"

Life gets more complicated when you and your friends start having romances. No matter whether your friend is the same sex as you or the opposite sex, two hard rules apply when it comes to their romances:

1. As a friend, you should not threaten your friend's romance.

2. Whatever you do or say, you should always keep your friend's well-being in mind.

You have a wonderful opportunity to build a new friendship here. Think of your friend's "significant other" as your brother or sister. You have a natural ally in enemy territory. Remember, friendship happens between people who have a lot in common. You have a lot in common: You share a good friend.

The Least You Need to Know

- A friendship with somebody of the opposite sex can be neutral, a place without competition or comparison, a place of freedom and comfort.

- Guys and girls have different communication styles.

- The typical Hollywood idea of friendship between girls and guys as the beginning of romance is not always true!

- Make it very clear to the world that you're not involved with your opposite sex friend.

- Casual sexual activity with friends usually ends up complicating matters and hurting feelings. Proceed only with extreme caution!

- Sometimes friendship between members of the opposite sex is too difficult. Be honest with your friend about your romantic feelings.

Part 3

The Challenges of Friendship

Friendship isn't always a bowl of cherries. Hold onto your hat, we're about to deal with the harder parts. In Chapter 9 I'll give you hints on dealing with the all-too-common combination of friendship and romance. Chapter 10 deals with a friendship's crimes; how to identify them, and how to cope with them. Since most friendships involve conflict, Chapter 11 is devoted to learning how to fight well and fairly. Chapter 12 is packed full of advice about helping a friend who's in trouble. Chapter 13, the final chapter, tells you how to cope with the end of a friendship.

Chapter 9

Friendship and Romance

In This Chapter

- From friendship to romance ... and back again
- The new relationship and your expectations
- Dealing with being dumped (or dumping)
- Your friend's love affair and you
- When your friend's in a bad relationship
- Hands off your friend's partner!

Welcome to the love chapter! Sometimes friendship becomes romance. This can be a good thing—the very best romantic relationships often start as friendship—or it can be a disaster, especially when you break up. This chapter takes you from friendship to romance and back again. We'll also look at how to deal with your friends' romances—especially if they're in a romance and you're not.

Face it, balancing friendship and romance is tough, but it's a challenge you'll be facing for the rest of your life. Like friendship's other challenges, learning to deal well with it now will make everything else easier later on.

When Friendship Becomes Romance

Your pal is your pal, and just because you're of opposite sexes (or, if you're gay, of the same sex) doesn't mean romance is inevitable or even what you want (review Chapter 8, "Guys and Girls as Friends"). But what if ... all of a sudden ... sparks do fly between you? Maybe you feel a surge of emotion inside you and realize that your feelings have changed, and your friendship may be on its way to being something much hotter.

Is It Mutual?

Just because you're seeing stars, feeling sparks, and generally getting mushy and romantic doesn't mean your friend is, too. Or maybe your friend is suddenly mooning over you. Do both of you feel the same way? If it's not mutual, one of you is bound to be hurt and disappointed. How do you know if the feelings are mutual? You may never know unless you ask, or make a romantic move. Think carefully before you decide to take the plunge, though. Once you've brought it up, you may find that the friendship changes, even if you both decide not to act on romantic feelings.

Just Between Friends

Friendships can survive Cupid's arrow, and many do every day. But in order to survive as close friends, it helps to be truthful about your feelings, no matter what they are. Your friend may not feel the same way you do, but he or she will appreciate your honesty.

Should You Tell?

Once you realize how you feel about your friend, you need to decide what—if anything—you're going to do about it. If you're feeling just a glimmer of romance, you may not need to do or say anything. Many friendships include minor romantic or sexual sparks. If they aren't the main event and you can't see them going any further, you might want to let sleeping dogs lie.

Here are a few things to think about before you hit your friend with the big truth:

- Don't rely on other friends to spread the word about how you feel. Tell the person yourself. Yes, it's scary, but having your friend find out through the grapevine is worse.

- Be prepared to be rejected as a romantic partner. Your friend may even feel so nervous about your feelings (even if they are mutual) that he or she may try to pull back from you—sometimes pulling all the way out of the friendship!

- Look for clues. Long eye contact, flirting, subtle touches, giggles ... all these can be (but aren't guaranteed to be) signs that your friend is feeling romantic toward you, too.

- Blurting out "I'm in love with you" or launching yourself physically at your friend can be really scary and even offensive. I recommend a more subtle approach. Engage your friend in an exploratory conversation: "Have you ever thought about us being more than friends?" Your friend may simply not have thought of you in a romantic way. Yet.

- Don't devalue the friendship. A good friendship lasts longer than most teen relationships.

True-Life Friends

"Romantic feelings come and go. Maybe if you wait a while, things might just sprout up. But don't push anything because that will make it uncomfortable."

—Sopheary, age 18

There's no right or wrong answer to the dilemma of whether or not to share your feelings. Only you can decide if you should go for it. Just be careful who you confide in; this is juicy gossip, so keep it to yourself or choose a rock-solid confidante.

Just Between Friends

Friends don't substitute for a romantic relationship, but neither does a romantic relationship substitute for friendship.

Unrequited Love

What if you let your friend know how you feel and your friend doesn't feel the same way? Or what if your friend tells you he or she has romantic feelings for you, and you don't share those feelings? Yes, this can be very hard on a friendship. If you two really care about each other as friends it's worth trying to sort out your feelings by talking about it. Getting over a case of unrequited love isn't easy. It's easier if you've got a friend to talk to about it. (No, not the same friend you're going nuts about!)

A Friendly Reminder

You may long to have a romance so badly that you choose the most available person to have it with—a good friend. Watch out! Your friendship is on the line. Make sure you are truly infatuated with the person, not with the *idea* of being in a romance.

A New Relationship

What if the answer is yes! Yes, yes, it's mutual, you adore each other … hearts and flowers … birds chirping … you're an item! You're not friends, you're a romance; and with this shift in dynamics comes new joys and new stresses. Romantically, the better you know each other as friends the smoother the romance will be. Talk about your changing expectations for the relationship. How serious do you feel about each other? Are you just fooling around? Will you be exclusive or will you both date other people?

Once you're involved, you'll need to think about the physical aspects of the relationship. Sex can deepen or cheapen a relationship. If you're in touch with what you want—and that includes physical intimacy—and your romantic partner feels similarly, sex will probably intensify your relationship. If one of you is less committed to the relationship than the other, sex can shatter feelings and the relationship. It's vital to be honest with your partner about what you want.

Maybe you don't feel ready to be sexually involved, or you want to wait until you're older. That's perfectly fine. Don't let anyone push you into any kind of sexual activity if you don't want to or if you're not ready. And of course, nonconsensual sex—when one person forces sex on another, also known as rape—is *never* okay.

A Friendly Reminder

Honesty about sex includes an open conversation about—and taking preventative measures against—pregnancies and sexually transmitted diseases (STDs). For advice and information, contact Planned Parenthood at 1-800-829-7732; www.plannedparenthood.org. A good lover takes care of him- or herself and his or her partner.

Just Between Friends

When it comes to whether or not to have sex, researchers say that teens are more influenced by their friends than by their parents.

The Big Breakup

The relationship has run its course. Maybe it's been a few weeks, maybe a few years. Either way, it's over. One or the other of you (or maybe both) wants to make a change. It hurts when your partner breaks up with you, even if you had the same idea. Getting over a relationship might feel like a minor disappointment or it may feel utterly devastating. How serious the relationship was generally determines how bad you'll feel and how long you'll feel that way. Yes, you will survive this loss. You'll feel better faster if you acknowledge how disappointed and rejected you feel. Let yourself be sad and angry. And don't isolate yourself. Now's the time to get back out there and hang with your friends.

True-Life Friends

"In high school I fell in love with my very good friend Greg. He didn't share my feelings, but we went out for a couple of weeks. When he told me he didn't want to be my boyfriend, I was devastated. It ruined the friendship. Years later, Greg found me on the Internet. Though we live in different states, we write e-mails, and recently had lunch together when he was in town."

—Ericka

If you are the person breaking up the relationship, you may have it easier than the person you are breaking up with, but it's still a very hard thing to do. This is especially true if you two were tight as friends before you got together. Both of you will get over it faster if you're kind and honest with your friend.

Can You Be Friends with Your Ex?

There's no rule that says you have to be friends with your ex. Sometimes feelings are too raw to move immediately back to friendship (if you started as friends) or into friendship for the first time (if you started as a romance). Regardless of who broke it off, listen to your instincts and trust your own feelings. You may simply need some time or distance away from the person.

The harder the breakup, the longer it takes to get back to friendship, if you ever do. Hurt feelings have to settle, jealousy has to fade, one (or both) of you may have to move on. But if you trust each other, like each other, and enjoy spending time together, there's no reason why you shouldn't be friends with your ex!

For teens, friendships are a lot more stable than dating relationships. And even though the feelings may be more intense (yowza!) between two people who are romantically involved, a good friendship is at least ... if not more ... important.

Just Between Friends

You and your ex have one strong thing going for your new friendship: the shared experiences you had when you were dating. You learned a lot about each other, and that can make you closer friends!

New Relationships and Your Ex

It's over. One or both of you has moved on to dating other people, and you're really friends now. Congratulations! You've achieved something special, something valuable. But there's a problem. Your new "significant other" is jealous of your friendship with your ex. He or she can't believe that things between you are really over, or maybe she or he feels jealous of what you and your ex once had.

This kind of jealousy is common and can be very destructive. Reassuring your new partner and being honest about how you feel can help. Your new partner needs time to feel secure in his or her own relationship with you. Remember, though, that it's your right to maintain friendships, even with someone you used to be involved with.

Your Friend's in Love

When a close friend has a romance, you're affected too. Maybe your friend isn't spending as much time with you, or you get to hear about dream boy or dream girl until you can't stand it anymore. Especially if you're not dating, or haven't been in love yet, it's hard to listen to your friend ooh and ahh and gloat and giggle. How do you cope?

- If your friend is in love and talking about it all the time, remember that he or she is in the throes of a very powerful emotion. She can't always stop, so try and be tolerant!

- It's hard to be the "third wheel," the single person hanging out with a couple. It's harder still if you don't particularly care for your friend's new partner. You don't have to feel enthusiastic about him or her, and you don't have to spend all your time as a threesome! Look for things to do on your own or with other friends.

- Let your friend know that you still want to spend time with her ... just the two of you. Friendship can accommodate love without being re-prioritized out of existence.

When Your Friend Is in a Bad Relationship

It hurts terribly to watch a friend in emotional pain or in a bad relationship, and the hardest part is not having any control over what's going on. Express your concerns about your friend's partner or the relationship, but don't expect to be listened to. Love's power blinds many people to reality, and your friend has to make his or her own choices. When your friend's relationship ends badly (as bad relationships often do), never say "I told you so." Bite your tongue! A good friend is there to help pick up the pieces and lend a sympathetic ear.

If your friend is in an abusive relationship, however, you may need to intervene and get some help. There's more information about this in Chapter 12, "A Friend in Need."

True-Life Friends

"Be there for your friends. Don't tell them that someone better will come along or that he was bad and yadda yadda, they don't need to hear that. Just listen. Input isn't always good."

—Sopheary, age 18

Hands Off: Friends Shouldn't Share *Everything*

Sure, friends like to share. But sharing a romantic partner is a bad idea. Yours isn't the first friendship to face this ugly situation. What about when your friend "steals" your partner (or crush)? Know that nobody can be "stolen" unless they want to be. Think about your friend's intentions. Is he or she really that good of a friend?

Maybe you're the one with that giggly feeling inside when you see your friend's significant other. You find yourself wanting to look good, sound great, and entice. You know he or she is off-limits, but you're in agony. These tips might help:

- Just because you're feeling passionate doesn't mean you have to do anything about it. Focus on your other interests and stay busy with other friends.

- Don't fool yourself into thinking that kissing your friend's partner (or even going out together) will help you "get over" the feelings. Actually, the more deeply involved you get, the deeper your feelings are likely to be. Stop before you start. Put the brakes on now!

- This kind of longing for somebody else's boyfriend or girl-friend is often a case of the grass being greener on the other side of fence. You've seen a glimpse into this person's tender side when he or she was with your friend, and you want it for yourself. Maybe it's the tenderness you want rather than the actual person. That tenderness exists in everybody. Wait and find your own person.

A Friendly Reminder

Messing around with your friend's relation-ship (and the reverse) can completely destroy a friendship. Don't go there!

Let's say despite your good intentions, it's happened. You've been a rat and gotten involved with a friend's partner. But you really care! Your dilemma is old as time, and it's a tough one with no one easy answer. You have to choose who is more important to you, knowing that friendships tend to last longer than romantic attachments in the teen years.

I can't tell you what to do, but I have some advice (and this advice comes straight from experience). The only way to keep your friend-ship strong is to be honest. Take the high road! Tell your friend what's going on, and deal with the anger and hurt feelings. If you're not honest, you're actually making things much harder for all three of you in the long run. You may lose a good friend, and you'll prob-ably feel pretty crummy about yourself.

Relationships started with this kind of tension rarely work out well. And you may not end up with the person anyway. (Is he or she re-ally worth all that agony?)

Just Between Friends

If you can talk about your feelings with your friend before anything happens, you'll have a better chance of saving the friendship. You'll also have a chance to really assess how much their relationship means to your friend, and set your priorities accordingly.

The Least You Need to Know

- Moving from friendship to romance is tricky, and not always worth risking the friendship over.

- Expectations are different in friendship and in romantic relationships. Keep talking about it!

- Both "dumping" and "being dumped" is painful. Kindness and honesty helps.

- When your friend finds romance, it affects you, too.

- A good friend helps pick up the pieces when a friend's relationship goes sour.

- Messy "triangle" relationships put friendships at risk and rarely last.

Chapter 10

Crimes Against Friendship

In This Chapter

- When one friend gives more than the other
- Where nasty behavior comes from
- Criminals and their crimes against friendship
- When is a friend not a friend?

Friendship, like any relationship that matters, can hurt. People make mistakes. In this chapter, we'll look at what causes a friendship to run into problems, meet the perpetrators, and focus on ways to turn poisonous pals into fantastic friends.

This chapter is not about ways to ditch your friends, at least not without trying to improve a bad situation. Even the sweetest friendships have their rough spots. Sometimes a great friendship is buried under some pretty nasty behavior.

The Uneven Friendship

Let's start with looking at differences in expectations, because here's where a lot of friendship's disasters start. Unfortunately, friends don't come with labels that say what kind of friends they're going to be.

Trouble strikes when you and your friend expect different things from the friendship, or when one friend consistently makes more of an effort than the other friend. When the friendship is one-sided, the person who's putting in more energy feels hurt.

When you're trying to assess if a friend is truly a friend, consider the following:

- Look for patterns of behavior. Screwing up once is often forgivable; twice is dubious.

- Intentions matter. (That's why we look at the reasons behind the behavior.) If your "friend" really doesn't care, neither should you.

If you're expecting more from a friendship than you're getting, or if you're putting in a lot more energy than your friend is, you should reassess your expectations. That usually means lowering what you expect from your friend. Try to see the friendship for what it is. There are good things there, too! And if you see nothing, it's time to move on and put your energy into a friend who will return it—with interest!

Just Between Friends

Be true to yourself and your needs. We all need to feel cared for. Listen to that little voice in your head and ask yourself if this friend truly cares about you.

But what if it's you? If your friend feels as though he puts in a lot more energy and time than you do, it's time to reassess your actions and expectations. What do you want from this friend? What kind of friendship? Do you have more to give? Do you want to?

The only way to even-up expectations and energy levels in a friendship is to figure out—together—that things are uneven. And the only way to do that is to talk about it. Bring it up! Once the situation is out in the open, it's a lot easier to resolve.

Emotions That Can Hurt a Friendship

Differences in expectations and energy levels in a friendship can lead to trouble, but actual crimes against friendship are far more serious. Most are based on insecurity and low self-esteem, jealousy, and envy. Actually, jealousy and envy are often the products of insecurity.

It helps to see that some bad behavior is driven by inner turmoil. Understanding bad behavior doesn't excuse it, but if you understand the root the bad behavior's growing from, you might be able to help your friend—or yourself—change it.

Insecurity and Low Self-Esteem

At the same time you're struggling to meet people, feel less shy, and be a good friend to yourself, your friend is, too. Insecurity and low self-esteem can kill friendships. A friend's clingy behavior or constant need for approval can drive the other friend crazy. It's important to separate the behavior from the friend. Your friend is not evil, his or her actions are.

Jealousy and Envy, the Green-Eyed Monsters

Jealousy, of all the human emotions, seems to have the worst potential for destroying relationships and lives. It certainly *feels* terrible to be jealous, and it feels bad when a friend or romantic partner is jealous of you. But jealousy is a very powerful teacher. When you pay attention to your jealousy, you can usually figure out what's truly important to you.

Envy usually has less to do with a specific person and more to do with what's wrong in your own life. When your life feels hard or you're disappointed in yourself, envy often comes creeping in. It's good to acknowledge when you feel envious before you turn it into a crime against friendship; sometimes just talking about it helps it disappear.

Meet the Perps

We're all guilty, at various times, of not being as good a friend to our friends as we could be. The negative behaviors that I tell you about in the following sections don't necessarily mean the death of a friendship, but it's important to identify them so you can deal with them.

A Friendly Reminder

It's tempting to drop a friend cold when you haven't been treated right. But before you do that, give the friend a chance and talk about how you feel. True friendship is worth fighting for!

The Guilt Tripper

The guilt tripper wants more from you than you are giving. He says things to make you feel bad and guilty without ever clearly expressing his needs. The guilt tripper is quietly convinced that he's not worth your friendship—and at the same time, he may expect more from you than you can or want to give. If you can talk about it together, you'll clear the air and be a lot further along in your friendship (and no, that doesn't mean meeting his every need)! Your friend needs to hear from you that he's asking you for too much.

The Cling-On Warrior

Got a clingy friend who wants to do everything with you? Clingers are insecure and not satisfied with their own lives. They're scared of being left out, or just plain left. Of course, this becomes a self-fulfilling prophecy; the more somebody becomes a cling-on warrior, the more you want to shake her off. It's hard to learn how to say "Give me some space" in a neutral fashion. The key is to realize how stifled you're feeling before you explode and blurt out something hurtful to your friend. Gently but firmly tell your friend how you feel. Said too roughly, your clingy friend might magically morph into the next perpetrator.

True-Life Friends

"It's great to be with your friend, but my friend Nicolette wants to live with me or something. She signs up for the same electives and even outside classes with me. Sometimes I just need my own space."

—Claudia, age 15

The "Why Me?" Whiner

Some people always see the gloomy side of things. Nothing ever seems to go right for them. And when things really don't go right, they can turn into real drama queens or kings, relishing the trauma, making you live it alongside them, calling you day and night. The "why me?" whiner misunderstands the role of friendship. Yes, a friend should be there as a shoulder to cry on, but you're feeding into the behavior unless you refuse to listen when the whiner starts in on the small stuff.

Sometimes, of course, the person really is clinically depressed and the whining is a cry for help (there's more on this in Chapter 12, "A Friend in Need"). Most of the time, though, your friend will benefit from a "no tolerance for whining" policy. You will, too. Ignore your friend, or change the subject to something more positive.

The Competitor

This friend (otherwise known as the one-upper) doesn't understand the difference between social comparison and competition. If you do something, she has to do it while juggling tomatoes. She's not great at listening to you or responding to your needs because she's too busy keeping score. The competitor flaunts her cooler shoes, her richer family, or the better grade on the math test. Once she starts comparing love lives with you (hers, obviously, is better), she's manifesting the supreme sign of insecurity. She's afraid that she'll never measure up to you.

True-Life Friends

"My friend was such a pathetic whiner. Nobody took it seriously and then he jumped off the garage at his Dad's house. He's okay, but we felt pretty bad, like, did we totally miss something?"

—Charlie, age 15

Is this friend a total lost cause? Not yet. A friend's got to have your best interests in mind. Give her a chance to prove that she does, by telling her to cut out the competition. If it doesn't stop, *then* it's time to cut and run.

The "Bad Influence"

The bad influence is the friend your parents warned you about. He's on the path to big trouble, and he'll take you with him, if you let him. Maybe he's into drugs or gangs, or he thinks breaking into a convenience store is "cool." He might lead by example or by pressure (there's more on peer pressure in a moment). Only *you* know what's best for you. Don't let anybody make your decisions for you. If a friend tries, politely but firmly tell him where to get off the boat. A real friend doesn't exert that kind of pressure on a friend.

The Control Freak

Are you familiar with the power-hungry friend, the one who's so afraid of losing control that she has to have everything her own way? This friend suffers from a lack of imagination and total fear of not mattering to you, and as a result, *you* get treated like the sidekick. Not okay. You're the star in your own movie. Standing up to this friend will probably get her to back down. It's tough, but you owe it to yourself! If this doesn't work you should give this "friend" the boot.

The Fair-Weather Friend

The fair-weather friend likes you and hangs out with you when it's convenient and when nobody "better" is around. He'll be your friend until the popular group snags him for a party; he'll make a date and break it if something else more interesting comes up. When he's bored or wants something, there he is again. If you're interested in maintaining a friendship of any kind with a fair-weather friend, try giving him a dose of his own medicine. Don't be so available. If he gets the message and shapes up, that's great. If not, know that he's truly insecure or maybe he's just not that fond of you. In which case, it's time to lose that so-called buddy!

The Lost-in-Love Friend

This version of the fair-weather friend doesn't *mean* to dump you now that she's in LOVE, but that's the end result. Love is exciting, and especially in the beginning, it's tempting to spend all your time with your new sweetie. If you're the friend thrown over for the new love, however, you'll feel hurt no matter how much you understand what's going on. Tell your friend she's treating you poorly and arrange for the two of you to spend some time together, without her new sweetie. Or give her some distance and spend time hanging out with other friends or doing things alone that you enjoy. (There's more specific advice for this situation in Chapter 9, "Friendship and Romance.")

The Hypercritical So-Called Friend

The hypercritical so-called friend is always putting you down; it makes him feel better about himself (or that's his intent, anyway). This kind of criticism comes from insecurity and makes you feel bad (which is just what this criminal wants). You don't deserved to be treated like this. Cool it with this dude.

A Friendly Reminder

When you've been done wrong, it's tempting to repay the "favor." Don't stoop so low! Dragging your own behavior into the mud will just make you feel worse and look bad. It's harder to rise above such ugly pettiness, but much more gratifying in the long run.

The Morally Reprehensible "Friend"

Prejudiced behavior (racist, sexist, or homophobic) and cruel behavior are huge red warning flags. Sometimes this kind of behavior arises from ignorance or the way the person was raised. Yes, by all means try to educate your friend, but be wary. A cruel, inflexible, or intolerant person is bad news and cannot be a true friend. Do you really want this kind of person in your life?

Your Friend the Gossip

Your friend the gossip is having a lot of fun talking about people, and who can blame her? You may even like this friend because of the gossiping. If he or she constantly has the radar out for good dirt, you might really benefit. On the good side, your friend is interested in people. On the bad side, she's insecure and not convinced she's interesting enough without using your secrets to entertain others. She needs a ticket to get into the ball and you're providing it.

The gossip excels at gently prying out juicy information. She has no sense of boundaries, no shame! On top of it all, for the gossip, the truth may not be interesting enough, and stories get embellished, exaggerated, and cross the line into downright lies. When this happens the gossiping has potentially devastating consequences for everybody involved. If you're a victim of hurtful gossip, here's how to cope:

- **Ignore it or laugh it off.** Take a tip from celebrities, who are used to this kind of thing. Gossip treated with a light and uncaring hand has a tendency to go away.

- **Don't play her game.** Spreading rumors about her will only add to the trouble.

- **Confront her.** If you can muster the guts to say, "Hey, that gossip you were telling about me? It's not true!" right to her face, you might be able to kill it. Of course, this only works if the gossip isn't true.

- **Embrace the gossip.** Tell it yourself. Talk it up. You'll soon bore everybody out of it. Gossip feeds on the secret, forbidden aspect. If you're totally open with it, it's not really good gossip anymore.

- **Get philosophical.** Hearing bad gossip about somebody else reminds you that everybody is human. Even the most gorgeous, popular, and seemingly perfect person has flaws. Of course, that's not a good reason to spread gossip about the person. Be kind. Gossip can be painful to the person gossiped about. Break the chain!

- **Wait.** Time heals all gossip. Pretty soon something else will happen to somebody else, and your gossip will be yesterday's news.

- **Keep her out of the loop in the future.** Don't confide in her; she's abused the privilege.

True-Life Friends

"Gossiping equals death, but everyone does it; it's part of human nature. Just be careful."

—Sopheary, age 18

Peer Pressure

Parents tend to flip out over the idea of peer pressure, and it's true that teens are definitely influenced by their peers. Peer pressure is insidious; it worms its way inside you until you're making decisions based not only on your own feelings and thoughts, but the feelings and thoughts of your friends. Real peer pressure is not the guys on the corner telling you you're chicken for not drinking that rotgut in a paper bag, it's also their little voices in your head telling you what you should and shouldn't do—even when they're nowhere in sight. This is the kind of peer pressure that's hardest to argue with.

The best way to avoid peer pressure is to discover your own wants, needs, and feelings (see Chapter 3, "Finding the Friend Within Yourself").

The Least You Need to Know

- Problems between friends can occur when expectations (and energy and interest in the friendship) are different.

- The best way to solve problems is to talk them over with your friend.

- Most crimes against friendship are based in insecurity, jealousy, and envy.

- Friends can whine, gossip, influence you in negative ways, and treat you badly. If you still want to maintain the friendship, identify the "crimes" and address them with your friend.

- Some "friends" are just bad news. You need to cut your losses and run.

- Real peer pressure comes when you're making decisions based not only on your own feelings and thoughts, but on the feelings and thoughts of your friends.

Chapter 11

Friendly and Unfriendly Fighting

In This Chapter

- Why fighting can be a good thing
- Dealing with your anger productively
- Effective arguing and problem solving
- Listening techniques that really work
- Talking so you can be heard
- The elements of a fair fight

Conflict and arguing are a healthy part of any relationship, including friendship. Here you are, two opinionated people who share some ideas but disagree on others. Good, constructive fighting—and I don't mean having a knockdown, drag-out fist fight here—can actually enhance your relationship. Bad, unproductive fighting can destroy friendships. So how can you effectively fight with a friend and have it be a positive thing? It's all about communication.

Why Do Friends Fight?

Friends fight over different ideas, opposing opinions, misunderstandings, crossed expectations, deliberate or accidental mistreatment, distrust, jealousy, and crappy moods. Sometimes friends fight because they're venting stress on each other. The problem isn't *that* you're fighting, it's *how* you're fighting, and what the outcomes are of the fight.

Some friendships are easygoing, and some are not. How "easy" a friendship is has nothing to do with its worth. Sometimes the best relationships are those where the participants have a lot of conflict. Friendships like these can be intense, alive, and very exciting.

Just Between Friends

Researchers estimate that a typical high school student participates in an average of seven disagreements a day.

When You're Furious

You've got a temper (we all do, although some people's fires are slower to light than others). Anger is a normal emotion. Don't fight against getting mad, work with your anger to resolve the problem. What's the most productive way to deal with it when your friend has done something or said something that's completely yanked your chain?

1. **Take a time-out.** When you're furious, your breathing speeds up, blood rushes to your face, your heart pounds. You need some time to get through your reaction to a place where you can respond more calmly. If you need to leave the room, leave the room. Return when you're calmer.

2. **Separate the problem from the person.** Getting beyond a mistake or an inconsiderate action is easier when you keep the action separate from the friend. You don't really hate

your friend, you just hate what he said or did. Your friend isn't a creep, she just did a creepy thing.

3. **Give your friend the benefit of the doubt.** People generally try to do the right thing, and people's intentions are usually positive. Ask what your friend was thinking (or not thinking) when he said or did the evil thing you're so furious about.

4. **Resolve the problem.** Your friend matters to you. Work to resolve the problem by talking about it with your friend and listening to what she has to say.

The best way to deal with issues that come up is one at a time, as they happen. If you let things build up, you're going to explode. If you let them simmer, they'll boil over. Some people find it easy to express their hurt and angry feelings as they come up. They find it easy to let those feelings go after talking about the problem. For other people, it's harder.

A Friendly Reminder

Sociologists say that it's not unusual for girls between 14 and 16 to have a rough time with same-sex friendships. Maybe it's because the issues are bigger than they used to be back when they were kids, or because it takes time to learn to argue constructively.

What Makes a Good Argument?

A constructive argument clears the air and resolves angry, hurt, or confused feelings. Your goal isn't to win the argument (after all, if you win, your friend loses). Your goal is to resolve the issues you're arguing about so that both of you feel heard and satisfied. In a good argument ...

- Both people get to express their point of view.
- Each person listens to the other person's point of view.
- A sense of respect and care shines through.
- You solve the conflict and come up with some resolution (or at least identify a direction to work toward).

There are four ways to resolve a problem. (And I'm not counting the arguments that one or both people walk away from. Those aren't resolved ... they're just stalemated.)

1. One person wins.
2. The other person wins.
3. Both people compromise (each gets a bit of what he or she wants and gives in a bit, too).
4. You problem-solve your way to a creative solution that both people can live with.

Number 4 is a win-win solution and the best resolution. When you're in conflict with a friend, try for a resolution that makes everybody happy.

A Friendly Reminder

Having your say is only half an argument. If you just dump and run, you're not arguing—you're spewing and ranting—and giving up on actually resolving the problem. Always try and talk it through.

Listen Up

Being a good listener is the most important part of resolving a conflict—and it's a skill that will serve you well the rest of your life. Let your friend get it all out before you say anything. Don't file your nails, change the oil in your car, or watch TV while you're listening. Focus all of your attention on what is being said. Listening and really *hearing* your friend's point of view does not mean you are giving up your own. You don't have to change your position.

When you listen, remember the following:

- No interrupting! Just listen. You'll have a chance to present your side of the story when your friend is done.

- Don't do the "Yes, but ..." thing, where you plan your counterarguments as you listen. Just listen.

- You can ask questions to clarify what you're hearing, but forget asking "Why ...." Ask "How ..." instead. "Why" usually feels confrontational and combative. For example, instead of asking "Why did you tell my mom that I failed math?" ask "How did she react when you told her?" Your job at this stage of the process is to gather information, not get into accusations and blame.

Here's a little communication technique you can use to improve your listening skills and resolve problems. It's called active listening. It works especially well when you're feeling frustrated by the conversation or the person.

First, focus your attention completely on the person who is talking. Listen to the person's thoughts and feelings until she is finished. Now tell the talker what she just said. Paraphrase her thoughts and feelings without putting your own interpretation on it. Ask her if you've represented her words and feelings correctly: "You say you told Mona I was a jerk because you were pissed that I was giggling with Jason in the hallway. Right?"

Let her correct you: "Well, that was just the final straw. I was pissed at you for getting all the attention in Drama, too."

Say it back again, with the corrections: "So you're upset because everybody, including Jason, is giving me a lot of attention."

Let her respond: "That's it, I guess. I feel totally left out."

Listening actively lets the talker feel heard and reduces the number of miscommunications. It helps you really understand what's behind your friend's words and actions. Now you understand her, she knows that you understand, and you're well on the way to resolving your problem.

Just Between Friends

Sometimes your argument isn't with your friend, it's with yourself or the world in general. If you're stressed out, take a walk, take a bath, or take it out on the soccer field. Then, if you still have a problem to resolve, bring it up with your friend.

Talk Effectively

Talking is the second half of solving problems with good communication. It's harder than you think to talk effectively.

When you talk with your friend about what's upsetting you or why you're angry, try to be as clear as you can. It's okay if you get emotional or cry when you talk about something that really matters to you. Many people regularly mist up when talking about something that's important to them. It shows your authenticity. People, especially friends, respond to realness.

How Do You Get Somebody Talking?

Sometimes it's hard to get a dialogue going. In *The Complete Idiot's Guide to Dating for Teens* (Alpha Books, 2001), Susan Rabens recommends the "statement-question technique" of conversation. If you're in a disagreement with your friend and are having trouble talking about it, this technique can work wonders. First, make a statement about what's going on: "I noticed we've been getting on each other's nerves all day today." Follow it up with a question: "Do you think it's because we're in finals and really tense, or are you angry about something?"

True-Life Friends

"In fights it's very hard for me to see the other person's point of view because ... well ... I always think I am right!"

—Alicia, age 18

Use "I" Statements

Another technique to resolve problems is to use "I" statements while you're talking. When you start a statement with the word "You" ("You always ..." or "You never ..."), the person you're talking to tends to feel accused. If he's already feeling defensive because you're not getting along or in a fight, he's not going to hear what you say and he'll probably just get angrier and more defensive. An "I" statement simply focuses on how you feel, what you think, and your needs, dislikes, or likes. "I felt like crying when I saw you throwing my poetry into the garbage" starts a dialogue. "You threw my poetry away!" does not.

True-Life Friends

"Compromise, and realizing that people don't always feel the same way as you, are always good."

—Alicia, age 18

Stick to the Here and Now

When you express something that's upsetting you, keep your complaints in the present and keep them specific. Lose the words "always," "never," and "should." Focus on the specific problem; don't blast your friend with a list of complaints and resentments from the past. "I'm angry because you went to the movies without me and I felt left out" is specific. "You always go to the movies without me! And last year, you went to Don's party when you knew I wasn't invited, and then you flirted with my old boyfriend, who you *knew* I still liked ..." is dropping a bomb on your friend's head and will do nothing to resolve the conflict at hand.

Having a Fair Fight

All this effective talking and listening is great, and it does work. But what if you completely disagree, your friendship is on the line, and you have nothing left to lose? Challenge your friend to a fair fight in which you resolve the conflict once and for all. And no, once again I don't mean coming to blows. You'll be using the talking and listening techniques I just taught you, but you'll both be using them with the specific idea of resolving a very big problem.

A fair fight shouldn't happen in the school bathroom between classes. You can't accomplish much in 10 minutes. You need time, and you need to be in a comfortable place where you won't be distracted. Tell your friend: "Hey, we really need to work this out. Let's meet after school in the park so we can talk." Don't bring anybody else along for moral support. And don't schedule it before a big swim meet, a final, the prom, or anything really important.

Just Between Friends

Friendship is both strong and delicate. A successful friendship balances conflict and cooperation.

Either person can begin—let's say it's you, since you initiated the discussion. Using effective talking techniques ("I" statements and keeping things specific and current), describe the situation from your point of view. Take as long as you need. Your friend should listen actively. No interruptions allowed! When you're done, your friend should paraphrase what you've said. You can correct her until you're satisfied that you've been understood. Then it's your turn to listen actively while your friend talks. Don't be surprised if she has a completely different point of view about the events you're fighting about.

Let's say you've cleared up misconceptions and now totally understand each other's point of view and feelings. Great! But you're not done until you've talked about what the fight felt like, what it feels like to disagree, and how it feels to either have resolved your issues or know that you're really on opposite sides of an issue. It's important to step out of the fight and get a larger perspective on it. Analyzing the situation with your friend will help your communication in the future. You start (if you started in the first place). Describe your feelings before, right now, and during the fight. Your friend should listen actively and then paraphrase until you're satisfied that you've been heard. Now it's your turn.

Once you've resolved your differences, it's time to talk about the future. You talk, then your friend talks. Explain your hopes for the friendship. If you've hurt your friend, apologize (and maybe make amends). Then it's your friend's turn. If you've both made mistakes, talk about what you can both do in the future to keep the problem from happening again. Some sort of nonverbal acknowledgment of the resolution, like a hug, will help finish off the discussion. Congratulations!

The Least You Need to Know

- Conflict and arguing are part of any relationship, and can actually make a friendship stronger.

- Anger is normal, but there are healthy ways of dealing with it.

- Listening without interruption is an important part of communicating effectively.

- Effective talking means using "I" statements and keeping your complaints specific and in the present.

- Challenging your friend to a fair fight, in which you both use effective communication techniques, can help you resolve a conflict once and for all.

Chapter **12**

A Friend
in Need

In This Chapter

- What to do when your friend is in trouble
- Helping a friend through depression and coming out
- Resources for depression, self-injury, eating disorders, and substance abuse problems
- Help for family problems, abuse, pregnancy, and STDs
- Taking care of yourself, too

You've heard the expression, "A friend in need is a friend indeed." This chapter is about the "need" aspect of friendship. Friendship isn't always easy, and it's especially hard when your friend's going through challenging times. One of the best things you can do for your friend is just be there for him or her. In this chapter, we'll look at some of these challenges. You'll get information, resources, and approaches for helping your friend survive and thrive (while still taking care of yourself).

When Your Friend Comes to You for Help

Teens are under a lot of stress just because they're teens. Hormones alone can stress you out, not to mention school pressures, family issues, money problems, and friendships and relationships. Sometimes life feels like it's on top of you instead of you being on top of it. Friends can help you regain control and feel better about your life.

But what about when it's your friend who's in trouble and looking for help from you? Teens very often feel closer to their friends than they do to their parents, so it's not surprising that teens in crisis usually turn to their friends for help.

Before you even begin to try to help a friend, it's important to recognize what you can and cannot do. Know when you can't help. Don't think you can always solve your friend's problems—you can listen, you can support, you can educate, and you can go for help, but you can't solve a crisis.

True-Life Friends

"My mother has been obsessed with suicide for as long as I can remember. There was one failed attempt that I witnessed which was traumatic, and plenty of other related trauma. So I shut down. I was not available."

—Terry, age 17

Take It Seriously

We've all heard the news stories from schools where deeply troubled teens (and in some cases, younger children) have suddenly "gone off" and become violent. In most of these cases, other teens had heard rumors or had an idea that something was being planned.

Stories abound of suicides who talked openly about taking their lives, and nobody took them seriously. Or the girl who told her friends about her bulimia but, since she wasn't losing weight, wasn't believed—until she ruptured blood vessels from vomiting. Don't think your friends are just fooling around. Take any and all threats seriously.

Get Help

You can't help your friend alone. If he or she has been threatened, harmed, or abused—either sexually, mentally, physically, or through self-abuse—or if you know that your friend's actions will hurt somebody else, you must *tell somebody* (a teacher, parent, guidance counselor, or other trusted adult). You may want to protect your friend, but if he or she is threatening harm to himself or somebody else, you cannot assess the risk of it actually happening. Don't keep it to yourself! Many schools have anonymous hotlines to report threats. In this chapter I included many hotlines, information numbers, and Web sites.

A Cry for Help

What do you do when your friend is depressed, coming out as gay, having family problems or school trouble, gaining or losing a lot of weight, hanging out with a bad crowd, pregnant, self-abusive, or destructive? This section describes some of the problems and issues you and your friends may be facing, and gives resources for getting information and help.

A Friendly Reminder

Here's a little phrase to remove from your vocabulary: "I told you so." It doesn't help, it doesn't make you look good, and it only hurts. Sure, you may think it—just don't say it.

When Your Friend Is Depressed or Suicidal

Everybody gets down, everybody gets blue, everybody gets bummed, but there's a big difference between feeling momentarily lousy and being clinically depressed. True depression is physical and chemical. As a good friend, you are likely to know when your friend is having problems. Talk with your friend and try to figure out what's up. When in doubt, share your concerns with a trusted adult. And remember that cries for help aren't always explicit. It's good to keep a lookout for your friends' problems, but don't blame yourself if you don't pick up on the clues. They can be very well hidden.

A Friendly Reminder

It's Goth "style" to romanticize suicide and death, but your Goth pal may or may not be kidding. There's a difference between romanticizing an idea and feeling desperate enough to do it.

Although support from friends can really help, it can't fix the problem if your friend is clinically depressed. It's time for a closer look if …

- Your friend's eating or sleeping behavior has suddenly and dramatically changed.
- He's less interested in his friends and regular interests.
- She doesn't seem to care anymore for her friends, possessions, pets, or other things that were important to her.
- His grades are slipping or he's skipping school.
- She seems distant or complains about stress but doesn't want to talk about it.
- He feels hopeless and hates himself.
- She has no energy and feels numb.

- He doesn't care about what he looks like or radically changes his appearance but doesn't seem happy about it.

- She talks or thinks a lot about death or dying.

If any of these symptoms apply to your friend, he or she may need professional help to deal with depression. This is far more than just the "blues." Encourage your friend to get help right away. A doctor can prescribe medication or talk with your friend to combat depression and help your friend feel better. Help is out there! Look in your local phonebook (in the front, under "Emergency Numbers") for the suicide hotline number, or get initial information from this source:

Girls and Boys Town National Hotline: 1-800-448-3000. This bilingual (English/Spanish) suicide hotline is available 24/7. They can help you get information for a suicidal friend, as well.

True-Life Friends

"My friend was suicidal. I wish there had been someone, A Wise and Trustworthy Adult, to tell. My mother didn't take it very seriously, or more likely, didn't know what to do. Who was I supposed to tell? Teenage rebellion means isolation from adults, so it really was a difficult situation."

—Jos, age 17

When Your Friend Comes Out to You

It's not necessarily a crisis if your friend comes out as gay, lesbian, or bisexual. On the other hand, homosexuality and bisexuality are not well accepted in many areas, so coming out may be difficult for your friend. He or she may face parents who are upset or even threats from peers. You can help by listening and supporting your friend, and understanding some of the challenges he or she may be up against.

Here's some information to keep in mind:

- Coming out is scary. Your friend needs support and a friendly, nonjudgmental ear.

- You may wonder why your friend wants to come out of the closet in a hostile environment. It's hard to "live a lie." Your friend's decision is a momentous part of claiming his or her identity; different people choose to come out at different times.

- If your friend is coming out in a hostile environment, he or she may face some real abuse. You can help by refusing to laugh when people make anti-gay jokes, verbally supporting your friend, or getting help if your friend is being harassed.

- If your friend is gay, it doesn't mean he or she is attracted to you sexually. The vast majority of the time your friend wants you as a friend, *not* as a romantic partner!

- Your friend is risking a lot to tell you about her sexual orientation. He or she may be frightened of losing your friendship. Be honest with your friend—and with yourself—about how you feel.

- If you feel uncomfortable with your friend's sexual orientation, talk with your friend about it. Express your concerns and beliefs. You may need to agree to disagree, but remember that your friend is still the same person as before.

Just Between Friends

Ten percent of the population is gay, lesbian, or bisexual, so it's likely that, at some point, you'll have friends who are part of that ten percent. You should know that a person's sexual orientation is a part of who they are; it's not a matter of choice.

Here are some resources you and your friend should know about:

> **The Gay and Lesbian National Hotline (GLNH):** 1-888-843-4564; www.glnh.org. GLNH is a nonprofit organization providing nationwide toll-free peer counseling, information, and referrals. They're open Monday through Friday 4 P.M.–midnight and Saturday noon–5 P.M. EST.

> **Parents and Friends of Lesbians and Gays (PFLAG):** 1-202-638-4200. PFLAG provides support groups and resources for the families and friends of gays and lesbians.

> **!OutProud!: National Coalition for Gay, Lesbian, and Bisexual Youth:** www.outproud.org. This Web site is full of resources and information for gay youth.

> **Lavender Youth Recreation and Information Center (LYRIC) and LYRIC Talk Line:** 1-800-246-PRIDE; www.lyric.org/resources.html. LYRIC is based in San Francisco but its resource list reaches all over the United States. The LYRIC talk line, open evenings Monday through Saturday, is a place for lesbian, gay, bisexual and transgender teens and youth to talk about anything and everything in a safe, confidential environment. It's staffed entirely by youth.

When Your Friend Is Self-Abusing

Self-abuse refers to injuring yourself by cutting, burning, or other means, and it's fairly common behavior among teens. Self-abusers feel so terrible that they actually get relief from injuring themselves. The relief is temporary, though. Then they feel, ashamed, embarrassed, and scared of what they're doing. Your friend may hide his or her self-abuse from you. If you suspect that your friend is self-abusing, share these resources with her:

> **SelfHarm.Com:** www.selfharm.com. This Web site offers free information about self-harming behavior, self-injury, self-mutilation, and cutting; as well as links to newsgroups, message boards, discussion groups, and chats about self-harming behavior.

Self-Abuse Finally Ends (SAFE): 1-800-DONT-CUT; www.safe-alternatives.com. This organization offers information about self-harming behavior, self-injury, self-mutilation, and cutting, as well as support groups, out-patient and in-patient therapy, and a resource list.

Disordered and Restrictive Eating Problems

Many teens, especially girls, have issues with food; eating disorders are at the extreme end of the "disordered eating" spectrum. Eating disorders are potentially deadly and not something that can be fixed through friendship. Your friend needs professional help. Your friend either has or is at risk of developing an eating disorder if she does any of these things:

- Thinks she's fat even if her weight is normal
- Diets compulsively and keeps a strict food journal
- Works out obsessively
- Constantly counts calories and weighs herself every day
- Uses diet drugs to stay thin
- Purges through the use of laxatives or vomiting

True-Life Friends

"I have one friend who's so particular about her looks, she won't eat in public. She thinks it makes her look like she eats too much; she thinks she looks like a pig. She stuffs herself at home."

—Arden, age 13

Here are some resources to share with your friend:

National Association of Anorexia Nervosa and Associated Disorders (ANAD): 1-847-831-3438; www.anad.org. This hotline, staffed by people in recovery from eating disorders, is open Monday through Friday, 9–5 Central Standard Time. ANAD is a nonprofit educational organization providing education and support to sufferers of eating disorders and their families. They provide suggestions and referrals to support groups, and can help you move from phone calls to action.

Overeaters Anonymous: www.overeatersanonymous.org. This 12-step program helps people whose eating is out of control. They have approximately 7,500 meeting groups in over 50 countries. The Web site gives information on the organization and can help you find a meeting near you.

Drug and Alcohol Abuse

If your friend is abusing either drugs or alcohol, you both need information and resources. Here are some places to get help:

National Counsel on Alcoholism and Drug Dependence (NCADD): 1-800-622-2255; www.ncadd.org. NCADD provides counseling and treatment referrals as well as information on alcoholism and drug abuse, especially for teenagers.

Alcoholics Anonymous (AA): www.aa.org. Alcoholics Anonymous offers a 12-step recovery program to help people who want to stop drinking or stay sober. There are no dues or fees. Members meet in small support groups. The Web site includes information on AA and a simple 12-question quiz to help you decide if you (or a friend) is an alcoholic.

Al-Anon/Alateen Information Service: 1-800-344-2666; www.alateen.org. Al-Anon, a 12-step recovery program, helps families and friends of alcoholics recover from the effects of having a friend or family member who's an alcoholic. Alateen is the division that focuses on teens. This information line can help you find a meeting near you.

Pregnancy and STD Information

If your friend thinks she's pregnant or has contracted a sexually transmitted disease (STD), she needs information immediately. These resources are a great place to start:

Planned Parenthood Federation of America: 1-800-829-7732; www.plannedparenthood.org. Information on birth control, emergency contraception, parenting, pregnancy, abortion, and STDs. Check the Web site for a clinic near you.

TeenWire: www.teenwire.com. TeenWire has great articles, interactive features, and information about sexuality and relationships as well as a great list of resources.

The National AIDS Hotline: 1-800-342-2437 or 1-800-344-7432 (Spanish); www.ashastd.org/nah/tty.html. Run by the Center for Disease Control, this hotline provides resources for the public. They can send you AIDS and STD information confidentially and free of charge. They also give information about testing and can help you find a testing site.

When Life at Home Is Unbearable

Life at home isn't always wonderful. If your friend is experiencing violence, neglect, or abuse in her home, she needs immediate help from outside sources, as well as your love and support (but you knew that!). In addition to going to school authorities, your friend can call any of the teen hotlines mentioned in this chapter, or try:

KID SAVE: 1-800-543-7283 (24 hours). KID SAVE provides telephone counseling, information, and referrals to shelters, substance abuse treatment, mental health services, sexual abuse treatment, and more.

Rape, Abuse & Incest National Network (RAINN): 1-800-656-HOPE; www.rainn.org. RAINN provides free confidential counseling 24 hours a day, seven days a week, from anywhere in the United States. You (or your friend) will be connected directly to a counselor who can help.

Your Friend's Trouble Is Your Trouble, Too

You and your friend are bonded, and when your friend is in trouble, it's a tremendous source of stress and worry and grief for you, too. You may find yourself feeling depressed (it's depressing to see your friend going through a serious problem). You may also find that you're incredibly angry! You might feel anger at your friend, at the world, or even at yourself. All of this is normal.

When your friend is in bad shape, don't get so involved that you forget to take care of yourself! Now might be a really good time to go back to Chapter 3, "Finding the Friend Within Yourself," for tips and suggestions on taking care of you.

True-Life Friends

"When a friend is in trouble, roll up your pants and prepare to stick your feet in the mud. Always be there for your friends, no matter what!"

—Sopheary, age 18

The Least You Need to Know

- You can't solve your friend's problem, but you can provide support and encourage your friend to get help.
- Threats of suicide, violence, and other behavior should always be taken seriously.
- Depression, eating disorders, and other problems often have warning signs. Watch for them!
- Help with problems like depression, drug abuse, and eating disorders is just a phone call or mouse click away.
- If your friend is in trouble, you need support and help, too. Take care of yourself and don't be afraid to ask for help if you need it.

Chapter 13

Friendship's End

In This Chapter

- How and why friendships end
- When friends grow apart
- Coping and thriving when you or your friend leaves
- Grieving your friendship's end
- Moving on

This chapter is about the end of friendship. Friendships end in different ways and for different reasons. Not all friendships are destined to be forever, and not all should. Every friendship has a life span. There are those rare friendships that last a lifetime. You're a lucky (and skilled) friend if you get a few of those. Other friendships run their course in a couple of months. In this chapter, we'll look at the ending of friendship—from growing apart, as a result of a problem that can't be resolved, and from physical separation.

Growing Up, Growing Apart

Think of friendships as "friend ships"—sailing ships that sail together for a while and then, as the tides change, drift away from each other. It's a gentle way of thinking about growing apart. As we grow, we change, in often unpredictable ways. The close friends you have this year might not be the close friends you have next year, as each of you explores different interests and moves in different directions. You might have less in common, you might develop differences in attitudes, you might just like different people. It's even possible you're just tired of each other, although this is generally either a symptom of something really wrong in the friendship or signifies that you never really got that close.

When friends drift apart equally, all's well. The trouble occurs when one person wants to hang on. There's more about grief and hanging on to a fading friendship later in this chapter.

A Friendly Reminder

Don't assume that you did something wrong or feel bad about yourself if a friendship fades away or ends. Friendships have a life span, and it's not anybody's fault. You may simply have less in common now.

Sudden, Explosive, and Definite Endings

When things go wrong with a friendship they can go *very* wrong. Friendships can end abruptly because of misunderstandings, disloyalty, differences in expectations, unresolved conflict, mistrust, jealousy, or a third person in the picture complicating matters.

But all of these crises happen within friendships that last, too. So what's the difference? What makes one friendship survive a crisis and another dissolve into tears, fights, or sulking followed by the sad realization that you are not friends anymore?

When there's a crisis within a friendship ...

- Both friends need to really want to solve the problem and continue the friendship.

- Friends who are uncomfortable dealing with real issues in the friendship may wait until there's a blowup over something un-related, and then use the blowup as an excuse to end the friendship.

- Clear communication with your friend can provide a way to resolve a crisis and save the friendship. (Go back to Chap-ter 11, "Friendly and Unfriendly Fighting," for communica-tion strategies and tips.)

Just Between Friends

Most friendships have beginnings, middles, and ends. Unfortunately, it's hard to recog-nize where you are in the cycle until it's over. Ah, hindsight!

When a Friend Ends It

You're not always in control of your life or your friendships. When a friend breaks off a friendship with you—especially if it's sudden or unexplained—you'll probably feel surprised, angry, hurt, or puzzled. Not all teens are emotionally ready to discuss the real reasons be-hind a friendship's breakup. You can ask your friend. If you decide to try to pursue it, here are some tips:

- Consider writing a letter to your friend expressing your feel-ings and asking him or her to write back or, better yet, to meet with you.

- Don't plead, beg, moan, or cling to your friend, or you'll make it worse. It's sad, but the one person whose shoulder you used to lean on, your friend, isn't available anymore. Find another source of solace—another friend or a wise adult.

● Grieve (more about this later) and then let go of your grief as much as you can. Focus on making new friends.

When You've Done Wrong

At times it's not the other person's fault the friendship is over. Sometimes it's not even a two-way street; you've blown it and you've blown it big time, buddy. Perhaps you haven't been a good friend to your friend. Or perhaps your "crime" was a single, unforgivable incident. We all mess up. It's best to apologize and face the music. Do the best you can to make amends. If the friendship is indeed over, it's okay to feel sad, but don't hate yourself. Use the opportunity to learn something for the next time. How would you handle it when faced with the same situation again? That kind of learning is invaluable.

Just Between Friends

You've blown it? Don't hate yourself. It takes time to learn how to sustain a relationship. We aren't born with friendship skills, and there's no School of Friendship we get to go to. We're on our own, learning how to make friends, how to keep friends, how to let friendship go when it's over. These are hard lessons, but important ones.

When You Need to End It

You may find yourself completely unhappy with a friendship and decide to end it. Perhaps your friend is too dependent on you or you're fed up with the criticism your friend's always giving you (see Chapter 10, "Crimes Against Friendship"). Think seriously about your reasons for ending a friendship. You might consider simply taking a step backward instead, making the friendship more casual and less intense. If you do need to end a friendship—and it happens—try to be honest with your soon-to-be-ex-friend about why you're ending it. It's not just for your friend's sake, it's for your own.

I have a couple of people with whom I ended my friendship abruptly, without telling them why. With my one friend, our expectations for the friendship were different and I was afraid to be honest about it. I felt my other friend was cruel to me, yet I didn't directly address the problem. If I'd simply told each friend why I was breaking off the friendship (without being mean), I could have held my head up higher and felt better about my friendship skills. As it is, I simply dropped them. I'm left with a sense of unfinished business. I'm sure they were left with that sense, too. I've used these experiences (and I'm coming clean about them now) as a way to learn more about myself and improve my friendship skills. I've learned about my tendency to avoid conflict, and I've learned that I feel better in the long run if I face the conflict. It's a powerful lesson.

True-Life Friends

"My buddy Neil and I had a big fight about something incredibly stupid. I don't even know how it started, but it kept going on and things were said and more things, and our friends got in the middle, and now we hate each other. I still feel bad."

—Nick, age 13

Moving On

Circumstances end many friendships. Maintaining a friendship is incredibly hard when you and your friend are separated, when you no longer live in the same place, if your parents won't let you hang out together any more, or after you graduate. While friendships don't always have to end (many simply change form), they often do. Here are some circumstances you and your friend might face, and some suggestions on how to cope with the changes.

When One of You Moves

When one of you moves out of town, your friendship will change, or it may end. Either way, if you've depended on your friend as a big part of your life, the separation will be difficult.

In some ways it's easier if you're the one moving to a new place. You'll face new, exciting experiences, with a whole new crew to get to know. On the other hand, moving is scary, and you really could use the comfort of a good friend when facing all those new situations and new people. Staying behind is hard, too. You're stuck in the same old place and there's a big hole where your friend used to be. On the other hand, at least you know lots of people to get you through the loss of your friend.

True-Life Friends

"My best friend moved away to another state. Our parents arranged for us to see each other over the summer—he came camping with us. It was fun, but it wasn't really the same. We're still friends, but it's too hard to constantly explain what's going on to be really close."

—Brian, age 16

Moving away from each other doesn't automatically doom your friendship! With phone, e-mail, and Instant Messaging, you can keep in touch with your friend (see Chapter 7, "Long-Distance and Virtual Friendships"). Here are some other things to consider:

- Close friends can go years without seeing each other and when they see each other again, fall back into the same speech patterns, rhythms, and comfort with each other as if only days had gone by.

- Be prepared for changes in each of you. You'll make different friends, have different life experiences and concerns, and learn different things. Yes, you'll change and grow—and that's a good thing.

- Ideally, you will see each other again. If the distance isn't too far, work with your parents to try to arrange a visit. Visits can keep a friendship alive (they can also be a strain, if you and your friend have drifted apart).

When You Graduate

High school is like a pressure cooker: It puts a bunch of kids in a pot, tightens the screws, heats it up, and watches things boil. It can be intense. Your friends in high school may be the most intense friendships you have in your life. What happens when you take the lid off a pressure cooker? If you don't let the steam out slowly, you'll have an explosion. That's why so many friendships tend to end after high school. People "explode" in all directions, to different colleges, different scenes, different majors, different looks ... and simply a whole different group of people to get to know.

A Friendly Reminder

A graduation doesn't feel gradual, even though you may have thought about it with excitement—or with dread, in some cases—for years. All of a sudden, it's over, and you're on to the next stage of life. It can be a shock!

Graduations are always bittersweet. They offer a chance to make a fresh start, meet new people, and change your life. They also mark an end to the routine you've known for years, as well as the end of many friendships, especially casual ones. After graduation you're all off to different things. Even if you're just graduating from middle to high school and your friends are going with you, your friendships will face big changes as you all meet new people and face a new environment.

Does leaving high school mean the end of your friendship? Absolutely not. High school creates many friends for life. But even if you and your best bud end up at the same college or living in the same place, know that your friendship will change. Celebrate and value what you had, but at the same time don't be afraid to let the friendship evolve.

When a Friend Dies

The worst loss of a friend is death. Not only do you feel the grief of losing a friend, but the complete unfairness and horrible tragedy of a teenager dying. When a friend dies, you lose a piece of yourself, and to make it even worse, in most cases, your grief may not be fully recognized by the community—after all, you weren't one of the family, you were "just" a friend.

Just Between Friends

The death of even a casual acquaintance can be deeply upsetting, but when it's your close friend, the experience can be devastating. You need support, love, and maybe even grief counseling to help you work through your grief.

Moving through grief is a subject much larger than this book, and I can only give you a few words of advice:

- Depression or feeling numb are common responses after somebody you care about dies. Don't try to get over your grief alone. Go to your parents or other trusted adult, friends, rabbi, priest, or spiritual leader for support.

- Short-term grief therapy can help you understand your confused emotions (and emotions are always confused after somebody dies, no matter how they die, whether by illness, accident, violence, or suicide).

- Know that your friend is an important piece of you, somebody you will never forget.

The Importance of Grief

No matter how a friendship ends, it's important to grieve the loss. Until you do, you will have a hard time moving on with your life. Because teens often feel alienated from their parents and other adults, because love partnerships aren't yet creating new families, friends step in to fill the emotional gap. We rely on our friends for a tremendous amount. Many teens say that their friends are like family. At the same time, our culture teaches us that we should rely primarily on ourselves; we don't fully recognize the power and importance of friendship. Yet human beings biologically and emotionally need to live in groups and depend on each other.

Losing a close friend for whatever reason can be terribly traumatic, in some cases more traumatic than losing a love relationship. And it's a trauma, stress, and grief that's often not understood or taken seriously. You need …

- Time to grieve, and grieve fully.
- Support from other friends and family. It helps to have others understand how hurt and sad you are.
- To know that you cannot replace a lost friend; he or she will always be a part of you. We're lucky that the human heart has such a large capacity for new friends!

Letting Go

Some people hang on to friendships after they're over; other people easily move on to new friends and new adventures. Whether you try to maintain old friendships or easily move on to new ones depends on your personality. If you're like me, you tend to hang on to friendships long after they've served their purpose. I still miss my friend Karen, who I met my first week of college. After a year, we drifted apart (although we kept in contact a while longer), but we were into different things, living different places, exploring different adventures. I'd love to see her again, but really, our bond came from a few very intense months together. I have no idea if we would even like each other any more.

Just Between Friends

Friendships forged in crisis and intense times have a magic of their own. Even when they fade away or end, you'll always remember your friend fondly because of what you shared.

Except in the case of a friend dying, when a close friendship fades you might still be friends—just a "lighter" version of the friendship. If you can let go of the expectation that you should still be as tight as you once were, you can enjoy the friendship you had, and feel excited to share brief times together when you do spend time together. The better you know each other and the more contact you have, the more likely you are to continue some form of the friendship.

Are endings forever? Well ... maybe! Friendships are like forest fires. They flame, they give off a lot of heat, and sometimes, just when you think they're out, a little gust of wind will stir up a hidden ember and whoosh, the fire's roaring again. You never know when—and where—you and your friend will meet again.

The Least You Need to Know

- Friendships have a natural life span.
- It's normal for some friends to drift apart.
- Use the end of a friendship as a way to learn something about yourself.
- Grieve the end of your friendship and celebrate what you had. It's sad, but it's important!
- Some people move easily from one friendship to another. Others have a more difficult time of moving on.

Check out
other
Complete Idiot's Guide® for Teens
Books

SPIRITUALITY

The Complete Idiot's Guide®
to Spirituality for Teens
ISBN: 002863926X

DATING

**The Complete Idiot's Guide®
to Dating for Teens
ISBN:** 0028639995

LOOKING GREAT

The Complete Idiot's Guide®
to Looking Great for Teens
ISBN: 0028639855

A
ALPHA

Arts & Sciences | Business & Personal Finance | Computers & the Internet | Family & Home | Hobbies & Crafts | Language Reference | Health & Fitness | Personal Enrichment | Sports & Recreation | Teens

IDIOTSGUIDES.COM

Introducing a new
and different Web site

Millions of people love to learn through *The Complete Idiot's Guide*®
books. Discover the same pleasure online in **idiotsguides.com**–part
of The Learning Network.

Idiotsguides.com is a new and different Web site, where you can:

- Explore and download more than 150 fascinating and useful mini-guides–FREE! Print out or send to a friend.

- Share your own knowledge and experience as a mini-guide contributor.

- Join discussions with authors and exchange ideas with other lifelong learners.

- Read sample chapters from a vast library of *Complete Idiot's Guide*® books.

- Find out how to become an author.

- Check out upcoming book promotions and author signings.

- Purchase books through your favorite online retailer.

Learning for Fun. Learning for Life.

IDIOTSGUIDES.COM • LEARNINGNETWORK.COM